CW00828257

MODELLING
The Great Western
Branch Lines

MODELLING
The Great Western Branch Lines

CHRIS FORD

THE CROWOOD PRESS

First published in 2019 by
The Crowood Press Ltd
Ramsbury, Marlborough
Wiltshire SN8 2HR

www.crowood.com

© Chris Ford 2019

All rights reserved. No part of this publication may be reproduced
or transmitted in any form or by any means, electronic or mechanical,
including photocopy, recording, or any information storage and
retrieval system, without permission in writing from the publishers.

British Library Cataloguing-in-Publication Data
A catalogue record for this book is available from the British Library.

ISBN 978 1 78500 565 7

Dedication
For my Father, Raymond Ford

Acknowledgements
The author wishes to thank the following: Michael Farr, Simon
Hargraves, Nigel Hill, the Bala Lake Railway, the Severn Valley Railway,
Didcot Railway Centre, the Bodmin & Wadebridge Railway, Crawley
MRS.

Designed and typeset by Guy Croton
Publishing Services, West Malling, Kent
Printed and bound in India by Parksons Graphics

CONTENTS

CHAPTER ONE

INTRODUCTION

The 'typical Great Western branch line' is the way that countless model railway layouts are often described. This only comes second to the term 'classic'. When applied to descriptions of a model, the reality and irony is that neither 'typical' nor 'classic' is an apt description for what usually follows, which can often veer worryingly towards the unrealistic and the twee. There is, of course, nothing wrong with these slightly twee creations, which can, and do, give a vast amount of pleasure to the builder and the viewer alike. The Great Western Railway (GWR) branch-line model can be quite emotive for these very reasons, creating equally reactions of joy and total derision.

The truth is that in model terms it has over time become regarded as something of a cliché, far more than other similar branch-line models, and has resulted in a stream of repetitive models that are almost carbon copies of earlier examples. These frequent statements of Great Western layouts being clichéd are somewhat unfair, as although the Great Western Railway models may well be more numerous, the accusations of twee and unrealistic can in reality be levelled at any similar model of any railway company, without exception. And as the real thing drifts back further and further into history, the copying of other models will surely become ever more prevalent, as this is all the research that most people will bother to undertake. This slim volume is unable to fill these gaps in research in anything like a full and conclusive way, but hopefully more than anything else, it will nudge the reader into investigating some of the history of the Great Western branch system in a deeper fashion than may have previously been the case. If this happens even in a small way, then the book will have been deemed to be a success.

The classic and typical Great Western branch engine in the shape of a 45XX Small Prairie Tank. The numbering of GWR locomotives is confusing, but each class is usually referred to by the initial number of the class even if that bears little resemblance to the number on the cab plate. Here, number 5572 rests at Didcot Railway Centre.

THE GREAT WESTERN BRANCH AS A SUBJECT FOR A MODEL

Why then is the GWR branch such a popular subject? There could be a number of reasons. The first is that more than likely to many people the GWR branches ran through some of the most beautiful scenery in the British Isles, although this could be countered by the fact that every British railway company was in the same situation. If this was a primary reason, models of the West Highland Railway in Scotland would outnumber anything else by ten to one. Secondly, it may be the attractive green locomotives with the gleaming copper fittings hauling chocolate and cream coaches, but in human terms we are fast losing anyone who can actually remember that scene in real life and much of the Great Western Railway's money was made hauling dirty coal trains out of South Wales and transporting goods toward and away from the ports of Bristol and the Mersey. The third and more likely reason is that not only was the Great Western the country's longest lived and physically largest rail company, invoking a certain local pride in those who lived in its area, but the model trade and press has pushed the Great Western like no other line throughout the history of commercial model production, making it almost the default entry point for any modeller coming to the hobby during the last sixty years. This makes it the most straightforward for the novice, as there is just so much available with a Great Western slant. It is only in the last decade or so that the other three 1923 Grouping companies (the London Midland & Scottish Railway, the Southern Railway and the London & the North Eastern Railway) have had anything like as much attention from the model manufacturers.

WHAT SCALE?

At the time of writing, there are some nine suitable ready-to-run (RTR) locomotives for a Great Western branch-line layout, and that's just in 4mm scale (OO gauge). There are a similar number of coach designs

Another classic in model form, the 14XX 0-4-2 tank. This is a Hornby model (ex-Airfix) shown here as it comes, straight from the box. The prototypes were originally numbered in the 48XX and 58XX ranges, but the 48XXs were renumbered after World War II to 14XX and the entire class is usually referred to in this way, even the pre-war examples.

and the list of suitable wagons in RTR or kit form is simply endless. All that from current new product manufacturers, without starting to access the buoyant second-hand market. The situation in N gauge is similarly good, with four or five locomotives to get you started, but a little less in the way of rolling stock. The range of locomotives in 7mm scale (O gauge) is greater, although these are in the main in kit form and are not necessarily aimed at the novice. However, there is no reason why someone armed with a basic toolkit and plenty of enthusiasm shouldn't try one of the excellent Springside Models locomotive kits for the scale. There is recently, though, a sudden push to produce RTR locomotives and wagons in the larger scale and the modeller with even a modest amount of cash could now view this as a good entry point. The general understanding is that 7mm scale is almost four times the size in area terms as OO, so much less is needed to make the same visual impact, though naturally there is a little more baseboard area required for even a modest layout.

All in all, there is no excuse for not building a GWR branch-line layout and every reason to feel enthused by the sheer avalanche of material that will pour out from your local model shop. In fact, it is more than possible to build the layout purely from commercial shop-bought items, especially as in recent years there has been an explosion in the availability of 'ready-to-plant' resin buildings … at a price. These buildings are somewhat expensive when compared to the equivalent plastic kit or scratch-built structure, so if finance is a concern, there are large savings to be made by doing much of this work yourself. However you wish to approach this and whatever your skill level, putting a GWR layout together is by far the most straightforward route to an attractive and accurate model branch line in any of the popular scales.

WHY A BRANCH LINE?

In historical model terms, branch lines always came in second place to the glamour and speed of main lines, but sometime around the late 1950s to the early 1960s there was a shift in the general approach. This was largely triggered by the hobby becoming generally cheaper to enter. Beforehand, it had been the preserve of those who were financially better off and the models reflected this. Much of the rolling stock consisted of high-value items made by toy manufacturers in Germany, or hand-crafted at great expense in the UK – definitely not the playthings of the lower-middle and working classes. Then three things gradually happened: the prices of the models came down; the hobby was marketed as something for the 'aspiring and upwardly mobile father and son' to do (a gender-specific ploy that would definitely be frowned upon today); and in Britain the scale shifted downwards from the usual O gauge to something closer to what we know as OO, making these newer small-scale models affordable to the masses. The young family could now afford the train sets, but did not necessarily have the available requirements in domestic space. The idea was put forward that the best way to proceed was to build a compact branch terminus. This could be worked up whilst you gained confidence and acquired rolling stock, at which point the layout could be expanded (presumably when you moved to a larger house) to the large main-line layout of your dreams.

The social-climbing aspirational desire of the post-war masses was not lost on the model-makers and the idea of the pure branch-line model gained a traction that has remained ever since. The unforeseen outside factor during this post-war period was the rapid closure of the prototype branches by British Railways at around the same time, further prompting interest in rural branch lines that before had been regarded as not worthy of notice. As the branches closed, so the interest in preserving them in model form grew. The final piece in the jigsaw was probably the work of one man, Cyril Freezer, editor of both *Model Railways* and *Railway Modeller*. He promoted the idea of the Great Western branch line as an ideal with almost religious zeal. The model trade recognized the trend, duly followed, and the cult of the GWR branch in model form was complete.

Many of these reasons for choosing to model a branch line still hold true today, to some extent more so, as the size of the standard British home steadily reduces. The 'build a branch – expand to a main line'

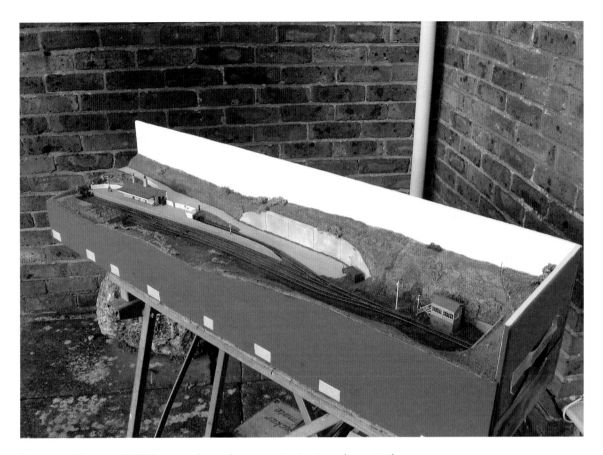

Here, an N gauge GWR layout shows how compact a terminus station can be. This model is built in the space of 45 × 12in (1,143 × 305mm).

course of action will certainly still work now, but whereas previously the result could be quite crude with little in the way of scenery around the railway, we can now easily produce a high-quality model that will far surpass anything that could have been produced in 1960.

The other modern development which could not have been foreseen in the early days of modelling has been the rise of the model railway exhibition as almost a hobby in itself. Every weekend, a travelling circus of modellers gathers in halls of various sizes all around the country to display their layouts. This also plays firmly against the idea of the large main line layout. These certainly do exist, but they are generally set up and operated by large clubs, are transported there by van and take a goodly while to erect. More common is the smaller group or individual who turns up in a private car with, what else, but the GWR

branch-line terminus in OO or N scale – the ultimate in portable model railways. In the 1950s and 1960s, the idea was centred around cost and fitting something into a small bedroom. In the twenty-first century, it is very much about what will fit into the family car; though in the end it all comes down to desire verses practicality.

WHAT SORT OF BRANCH LINE?

So let's assume that you have decided on a branch-line model and also plumped for the Great Western as the company, but what sort of branch do you want? Many of the answers to this will be expanded upon later in the book, but here are a few initial ideas. Due to its size and longevity, the GWR was highly diverse. The usual way of thinking is to build a branch terminus station with a platform, a goods

This Kitson-built 0-4-0 was absorbed into GWR stock when it took over the Cardiff Railway, where it worked the lines around the docks in the city. The GWR owned many such small shunters, built for and used in similar circumstances.

shed, an engine shed and a signal box. Bear in mind, though, that this was far from a standard set-up – many termini did not have engine sheds, some had only rudimentary goods facilities, while a few barely even had platforms. The reason for this is that the GWR acquired several independent and minor lines over the years and these were far from consistent in their build and shape, making the design of branch stations far from standard.

An alternative idea is to ditch the terminus station plan altogether and model a through station on the branch. This creates an entirely different set of operational requirements, as nearly all the traffic is passing on to somewhere else. There were also 'goods only' branches (or a short branch serving a quay), requiring no passenger stock at all aside from

a workman's train. The locomotives would be small and the focus would be on moving multiple wagons. An extension to this could be fitted in the shape of a single industry branch such as a quarry or a mine. Again, no passenger timetable would be required, but, for example, the traffic would be coal outward and empty wagons/stores/machinery inward. Due to the weight of trains, the locomotives could be quite large and would get you away from the 'small layout = small locomotive' mindset.

Lastly, there is an historical angle. Most model GWR branch layouts tend to be set firmly in the mid-1920s to World War II period, but if you were to drop this dateline back ten or twenty years, things start to look quite different, featuring outside-framed locomotives with open cabs, Crimson Lake coaching stock and even red-oxide wagons with heavy timber framing. Travelling back into the nineteenth century would give an entirely different view and you could even take on the challenge of the Great Western's broad gauge, of which more later in the book. This very lengthy possible timescale makes the Great Western unique, as no other British railway company existed with unbroken working and management structure from the early Victorian age through to World War II.

PLANNING YOUR LAYOUT

All of this can involve a large degree of planning and careful study. You may, of course, just lift a printed plan out of a book or a magazine and run with it exactly as presented. This approach will often work well, but bear in mind that some paper plans do not allow quite enough space, so do check that it will work before you start building. Many a layout has been abandoned through not building a simple mock-up with a few points and crude card buildings to establish that the plan will actually do what it suggests. Also, most published plans are already physically compressed for the modeller and will probably not take any further reduction.

Unless you are very confident, be careful not to overreach at this stage. A small, fully worked-out layout plan that is able to be finished in a reasonable amount of time is better than a grandiose room-filling idea that will never have a chance of getting done. The key point is often to work out as part

Bob Vaughan's highly detailed and compact OO layout 'Condicote'. Note that almost everything in this scene save the platform is a commercial item, readily available at all model shops. This demonstrates that even though most are not marketed as Great Western, with skill and practice a very convincing scene can be achieved and will reflect a GWR atmosphere with only small amounts of visual information. Only the van, the coach body and the pagoda building are GWR designs, yet the viewer is fooled into thinking the whole is typical.

Tip

Spend plenty of time deciding what you want to achieve in terms of scale, period and size of the overall project before you buy too much or start work on a layout.

of the scheme how much time you realistically have available, as this is probably more important than the layout plan itself. It doesn't matter how many or how large a plan you dream up in your head during your working or commuting hours. If you only have twenty minutes of spare time a day outside of work and family commitments, then a big layout simply will not get done. It is a far better policy to start small, pace yourself, and build something that can be regarded as finished within a reasonable amount of time. A project that is likely to take longer than a year to complete will quickly lose inertia and will become a millstone, rather than a pleasure.

HISTORICAL PROTOTYPE RESEARCH

Unless you are desperate to get started straight away, doing a little prototype research will be time very well spent. This could be nothing more than a little casual browsing through some of the mainstream model magazines such as *Railway Modeller* or *Model Rail*, or it could be something much more academic and organized. A very brief general history of the GWR follows in the next chapter, but as a gentle preamble there are a couple of points to consider. Firstly, the layouts in magazines have a habit of replicating themselves and this is where the problem of the GWR branch line being a cliché tends to emanate from. While it's wrong to criticize other people's modelling work, it is often hard not to wonder if the builder has looked outside the modelling catalogues and magazines at all, such is the repetition of ideas. The defence for this is that in many ways the GWR is just as much an historical experience as, say, the Tudor period, so other people's models tend to become the pattern.

We are now at the point in time where there are few who can remember the pre-World War II era, so we are reliant on contemporary film footage and photographs in exactly the same way as we are reliant on documents and artefacts from the Tudor 1500s – and that is where most of the problem lies. We readily accept that everyone carries some sort of camera now, but although cameras were available in the 1920s, they were still very much a luxury item. Add to that the high cost of film compared to the throwaway digital format, and the subject matter chosen by the photographer became much more prone to natural selection. In other words, if you were going to photograph a train, it was likely to be a big, glamorous example and not a small, grubby train on a branch-line goods service. Therefore, what does exist photographically in spades is the record-breaking express, but much less of the ordinary working branch-line trains.

The suggestion for the novice is to start collecting some of the picture-album books that refer either to the GWR as a whole, or specifically to the area being modelled. The second-hand market often turns up books from the publisher Bradford Barton. These are useful, as they are comparatively contemporaneous with the end of steam in the UK. However, this can offer up traps, as while branches were notorious for keeping the same running style beyond World War II, it is usually only the locomotives (albeit reliveried for British Railways) that remain from pure Great Western days. There was a dramatic change in wagon design post-war, and often as not the coaches too were upgraded from the 1930s types, so a little thought is required before taking the photographic evidence as typical for the pre-war period. The newer versions of the Bradford Bartons are the books from Middleton Press, which deal with the railway system almost line by line. These do occasionally feature pre-war images, but they are mostly very up to date and therefore useless for our needs. The whole process is one of sifting through material and discarding that which has no relevance. In essence, it is pure historical research. Lastly, it is worth picking up *Great Western Railway Journal*, which is available quarterly from larger newsagents. It does get very detailed at times with regard

Tip

Study the prototype first and do not base your layout purely on other people's models.

to the written work – possibly much more than the novice will require – but the photographs are high quality and very useful.

The main thing that the novice modeller is looking for is the make-up of the trains in given situations for branch traffic, for instance: are the trains loco-hauled or push-pull (the locomotive hauling the train one way, then pushing on the return journey)? Are the passenger trains 'mixed', with wagons added? What sort of goods traffic is being carried, and so on? Also,

the layout of the station buildings and trackwork should be noted. Rarely is it exactly as many of the model plans would have you believe, as these are often swayed toward using commercial track units. As obvious as it sounds, the key here is that the real railway company laid out a station to make the railway as efficient and cheap to work as possible, whereas the modeller in the main aims to add operational interest and complication to what would possibly be a very simple and straightforward working practice. This aspect will be dealt with toward the back of the book, but it is something to think about as your planning evolves.

ATMOSPHERE

What we are probably trying to gain overall here is atmosphere. This is a slippery beast and often hard to get hold of, but it can be done with a little thought.

The modern preservation scene at Bodmin – 57XX pannier tank shunts its train. Note the open hatches and the riding position of the fireman – a long way from most model crew poses.

Again, there are questions to ask: Is the railway/station site rural or urban? Not all GWR branches were set in leafy countryside. Is there a single traffic that needs a specific set of buildings, such as a dairy? Are there one or more platforms and are they long or short? Several of the classic lines (there's that description again) started their lives as light railways, such as the Culm Valley line, and had very basic platforms which were no more than 200ft (61m) long. Others that catered for big holiday crowds, such as those in the West Country, had much longer platforms to cope with large trains disgorging many passengers. These questions need to be asked quite early, as it may affect how you do something. If you already have a picture in your mind's eye of a tiny tank engine pulling a couple of four-wheel coaches, then something like the Culm Valley or the Tanat Valley with their small, simple stations may be your ideal prototype, but if you want a more main-line feel with longer trains and larger engines, then that is going to look ridiculous in the same setting – that would need a much more passenger-heavy situation and vice versa. The railway traffic and the shape of the station site tend to go hand in hand.

The 'typical and classic' atmosphere beyond the trains is somewhat easier to achieve and most of it can be done with a lick of paint. This applies to any model railway really – simply study the company colours of the paintwork on the buildings and the colour of the station signage and copy it. This will get you most of the way there. In this case, the overriding scheme is to use, in the GWR's terminology, dark, mid and light stone. The dark stone is a red chocolate brown, not dissimilar to the brown used for the coaches, and the light, a cream with a hint of pink in it. However, these colours were open to a degree of local interpretation and the further away from Paddington and the more out of the way the buildings were, the more variants in these colours could occur; often as not, the light stone morphed into a muddy cream. Signage for most of the system was usually white lettering on a black background, although again there was quite a bit of local variation.

This attention to colour and detail should provide both you and the casual viewer with an instant rec-

ognition of the railway company. The rule of thumb is always to be able to recognize the place and company before the trains arrive. If your model railway achieves this, you will have succeeded in your efforts.

GEOGRAPHY AND GEOLOGY

One more thing to consider is a loose sense of geography and geology. Urban scenes are a case apart, but if your layout is country-based, it is almost essential that you consider the lie of the land: Is it rolling Devon hills? Fearsome bleak Welsh mountains? Or perhaps the much flatter Thames Valley? Even with a relatively small layout, this can be suggested quite quickly with ground contours, reinforced by a suitable backscene. Having a few visual pointers can help the trains 'sit comfortably' within their surroundings, making the layout feel all of a piece rather than a set of unrelated, disjointed items that look to be thrown together.

TAKING INSPIRATION
FROM PRESERVED LINES

The Great Western modeller is lucky in the respect that there are several well-organized preserved lines which are either ex-GWR branch or main lines. A few of these are some of the longest in the British Isles, such as the West Somerset Railway and the Severn Valley Railway, down to short demonstration lines like the Didcot Railway Centre. All of them are very welcoming and have a good range of ex-GWR locomotives and rolling stock to study. But these preservation lines, however well run, can only hint at the sort of operation that would have taken place on the real Great Western. There are no connecting services at junctions, no porters pushing barrows full of luggage and no slow-moving goods trains clanking through the station during quieter mid-morning periods.

Nevertheless, preserved lines are fine places for not only an entertaining day out, but somewhere to do a little research and to gain an insight into branch-line working. For although many of these preserved railways are sited on old main and secondary routes,

The approach to St Ives. The steam has long gone, but the service still remains. Replace the modern 150 unit and it is still a GWR scene from a branch worked for many years by prairie tank engines and long passenger trains.

The preservation scene is full of interest and there are gems tucked away from the main theatre. This 2-8-0 tank was designed by the GWR to haul heavy coal trains out of the South Wales coal fields and stands in the sun awaiting attention. Note the correct, but unusual, lettering style typical of the South Wales locomotive sheds.

Tip

Ensure that you always have a camera with you on these trips to record as many small details as possible. Not just the locomotives, but lamps, platform seats, buffer stops and other miscellaneous details. These are rarely recorded by the casual and family visitor, but will add to the atmosphere of your layout. The small amount of research undertaken around such items will add to the pleasure of building a layout.

Tip

Chat to your local retailer about the different track systems before finally deciding on which one to settle. Most new RTR items will run on the finescale track ranges, but some of the earlier pre-1990s models, such as those made by Lima, have wheel profiles that are too large. If you plan to use this age of stock, sticking to the standard Hornby/Peco code 100 rail is possibly your only option.

the working is much closer to branch-line routine, with the same rake of stock drawn back and forth and with uncoupling and running-round taking place at each end. This preserved-line atmosphere may actually give an alternative base for a model rather than the usual pre-World War II historical approach – one that is still a GWR branch line, but set in the present day, using clean and polished preserved rolling stock.

SCALES AND GAUGES

At some point during the planning process the question of scales and gauges will arise. We will start with the 4mm scale, of which OO is the most common. This is actually a track gauge (the measurement between the rails) of 16.5mm. All the main track manufacturers such as Peco and Hornby use this as standard and they are largely interchangeable with each other, though there are even variations within this, with different ranges with marginally different rail heights and cross sections. If in doubt, it is probably wise to stick to the standard Peco Streamline Code 100 range, which also matches the Hornby track.

There are also two further 4mm scale gauges: P4 (Proto-four), which is exactly accurate at 18.83mm gauge, and EM (18mm) at 18.2mm gauge. Both of these require a certain level of skill and need in the main to have at least some of the track built by the modeller and the locomotives and rolling stock adjusted to match. It has to be said that there is a degree of

snobbery surrounding these last two. Yes, it is trickier to accomplish, and yes, it is more accurate, but to be quite honest, 99 per cent of the population is unlikely to notice. The advice to the novice is to stick (at least initially) to OO gauge, build your first layout and worry about hyper-exact track gauges later. All the RTR models you will buy are designed for this gauge, so you will avoid an unnecessary set of problems. That is not to say that the more ambitious novice could not achieve a good result by taking this path, but just that it will take more time and if you want to make adequate progress over the mid-term, using OO for a first effort would probably be the safest route.

Below 4mm scale is N gauge. This is nominally (but fractionally larger than) 2mm to the foot, so half the size of OO in linear terms, or 25 per cent of the total area. Again, there are several track systems to choose from, the most easily available being Peco. Moving up we come to O gauge or 7mm to the foot, with a track gauge of 32mm, which is also available from Peco. Most will plump for the popular OO, but aside from the three given here, there are several 'in-between' scales such as 3mm scale or the old imperial measured S scale, which is somewhat larger than 4mm scale.

USING THIS BOOK

Following the next short history chapter, the book is broken up into sections dealing with a particular aspect of Great Western Railway branch-line model-

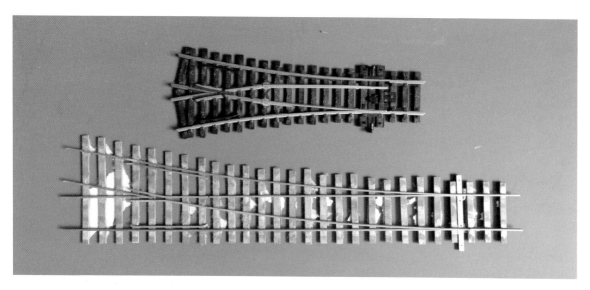

A comparison of two 4mm scale points (turnouts). The upper item is a very short Y from Peco, the lower is a medium-length right-hand unit in EM gauge (18.2mm). The Peco point is essentially made for the 3.5mm scale (HO) market, but has been sold as a flexi-scale item for OO for decades. Until very recently, all commercial OO trackwork was made with this market in mind.

ling. These are not necessarily meant to be read in order – more to be picked at as the fancy takes you. They are very loosely graduated in difficulty within each chapter and there is a certain amount of technique crossover between projects, but that doesn't mean that you couldn't start with the trickier sections if that suits you.

There are no hard and fast rules with any of the projects. They are purely suggestions and all of the techniques are easily transferable to other similar items and, in the main, to other scales as well. Putting a plastic wagon kit together in 4mm scale as described here will transfer directly to a similar vehicle in 7mm scale. The model railway trade is notorious for suddenly taking a product off the market and some of the products used here may not always be available all of the time. It is safe to say, though, that due to the popularity of the subject, it is fairly certain that a new and similar item will rapidly become available.

Notes: The term 4mm scale should be taken to mean OO scale from this point on. The acronyms GWR or just GW (Great Western Railway) and

Tip

If a product is out of circulation it is often worth searching the Internet and/or trying an auction site like eBay for a hard to find item. Similarly, model railway exhibitions are a goldmine of older second-hand kits and bits which are all perfectly serviceable and often quite cheap if you are prepared to rummage a little and take a gamble on all the parts being included.

RTR (ready-to-run) will also be used throughout the book from this juncture. Any other acronyms will be explained as they are introduced.

Metric measurements are given where appropriate, but imperial measurements are used freely, as these are historically what was referred to at the time, for example vehicle chassis lengths are almost always referred to in imperial terms of feet and inches, and it would be churlish to try to fight against this standard terminology.

CHAPTER TWO

SELECTED HISTORY

The history of the GWR is not only the longest in British railway terms, but, as a consequence, is one of the most complex. The following chapter is really only designed as a small snapshot of some of the more relevant parts of it. If the reader wishes to dig further there are many books on the subject – some running into several hefty volumes, most of these dealing in the minutiae of locomotive development and in company legal movements, Acts of Parliament, land squabbles and takeover bids. While this will all be fascinating to the serious student of British railway history, it is not necessarily important here for the modeller of GWR branch lines. The hope is that by touching on a few selected periods and developments relevant to the GWR branch line, the reader will be inspired to research more and consider some different options to model. It also goes without saying that there have been probably more books written on the GWR than any other railway in the world. Specifically, for the branch-line modeller, Paul Karau's *Great Western Branch Line Termini* is a fine place to start and covers the central and south-western dead-end branches, but any of the single-line history books such as those published by Oakwood Press are also a good starting point.

BEGINNINGS

The Great Western Railway Bill was passed by Parliament in 1835 after a decade of discussion. This was to enable a line to be run from London to Bristol and had been the brainchild of a group of merchants from the latter city. This initial main line was built piecemeal and eventually opened in its entirety in 1841, connecting to the Bristol & Exeter Railway and thus allowing a train to run from London through to

A Bristol & Exeter Railway boundary post.

Section of broad-gauge track recreated at Didcot Railway Centre. Note the different design to standard track, with the flat-bottomed rail being laid directly on to longitudinal timbers and widely spaced transom timbers linking the two sides.

the West Country coast at Bridgwater in Somerset. However, it does not quite resemble the line today, in that the track was built to a gauge of 7ft ¼in (2,140mm). This was not unique to the GWR, as the gauge was adopted by several connecting railways, including parts of the London and South Western Railway, which was to cover quite a proportion of the south-west of England. Several of these lines, such as the Oxford, Worcester & Wolverhampton Railway or the South Wales Railway, were built in conjunction with the GWR. Others, such as the Oxford & Rugby Railway, were built by the GWR through subsidiary companies. Lines were also built by small independent companies, often funded by local business, but operated using GWR rolling stock. Most of these company names have now disappeared into history and as they were gradually swallowed up

by the parent GWR, they have generally come to be regarded as one and the same. This is where the novice can be confused, as the GWR is often portrayed as an homogeneous whole, when in fact it was the sum of many parts.

The choice of the wider gauge was taken by the man who is probably Great Britain's most famous engineer, Isambard Kingdom Brunel. It would be fair to say that there is no other name that is so recognizable to the general public even today, not just for railways, but for shipping and other civil engineering. Though he worked for other railway companies, his name will always be linked primarily to the GWR, with seemingly a hand in virtually the tiniest item of architecture. The choice of the broad gauge, as it was known, over George Stephenson's standard gauge of 4ft 8½in (1,435mm) is generally reasoned as giving a better and smoother ride. This was, after all, a line designed not only for goods, but for fast passenger traffic. Conversely, Stephenson's narrower gauge was the result of picking the best measurement for colliery wagons to ride on – passengers were not immediately considered – and it may indeed trace its roots back to Roman cart width and wheel gauge.

Note: GWR texts often confusingly refer to the Stephenson (4ft 8½in) standard gauge as 'narrow gauge' to differentiate from the term broad gauge, whereas in all other places narrow gauge is taken to mean one which is less than the Stephenson standard gauge, such as 2ft or 3ft gauge.

The problem with the broad gauge was that as the system expanded and met with other lines, these were not always the same broad gauge. In fact, as time went on the GWR recognized the issue and either built new lines to standard gauge (no broad gauge was laid after 1874), or laid a complex web of mixed-gauge track that combined the two. The main problem was trans-shipment at points of gauge change – passengers had to detrain and join another with their luggage, which was inconvenient, but goods traffic had to be manhandled from one train to another, often in large trans-shipment sheds, which not only required a vast amount of manpower, but took up quite a period of time, incurring extra cost to the company. It was therefore decided that standard gauge should be adopted throughout the system and all broad gauge running ceased in 1892.

EARLY ROLLING STOCK

Most of the early locomotives built for the GWR passenger work were of the 4-2-4 arrangement, with one pair of large driving wheels in the centre and

Bristol & Exeter Railway 4-2-4 No. 44.

Replica 'Iron Duke' with two typical early four-wheeled passenger vehicles.

two pairs of carrying wheels fore and aft, although there were some oddities built along the development process. In addition, 'goods' engines were often only 0-4-0 or 0-6-0 arrangement. All of these early designs were relatively lightweight with small boilers and generally used coke as the heating fuel and not coal, which was not used until 1857.

Coaches were initially four-wheeled and six-wheeled, all with styling closer to stagecoach design for the higher class vehicles and open wagons with plank seats for the lower classes. There were also 'carriage trucks', in which the wealthy could travel to Bristol in their own road carriage strapped to a flat wagon, or at the very least travel in another coach while their vehicle was transported behind.

THE REMARKABLE WEEKEND GAUGE CHANGE

What happened next is one of the remarkable railway feats that has become part of historical folklore. The last broad-gauge train travelled into London on 21 May 1892 and standard-gauge rolling stock had previously been sent west on broad-gauge flat wagons. Over the next two days, 177 miles (285km) of broad gauge track was relaid to standard gauge by an army of permanent-way workers, with the result that standard-gauge trains ran from London to all points from 23 May. Even taking into consideration the lower safety standards of the age, the breakneck speed in which this was achieved compared to the simplest piece of road repair today is nothing short of amazing. The tidy-up work of sidings and secondary lines continued throughout the year and aside from stock storage sidings at Swindon, the broad gauge had ceased to exist by the end of the year.

MODELLING THE BROAD-GAUGE INFLUENCE

You may be thinking that this discussion of broad gauge is not really relevant to the novice, and you would be mostly right. Modelling the GWR broad

Tip

If you are considering basing your model on one of the earlier lines, do a little research and establish the original gauge of the area, then construct the buildings and bridge spacing accordingly.

gauge is a highly specialized part of the hobby, supported by the Broad Gauge Society, and is probably not ideal for a first attempt. What is relevant is how it affected the GWR in general and in particular our branch-line subject. Aside from the main lines, many of the minor and adjoining branches were also built to broad gauge and consequently displayed the same characteristics as the rest of the system. Of course, you cannot run a broad-gauge train on a standard-gauge railway – not only are the tracks wider, but they also force the structures around them further apart. Therefore, pairs of platforms are more distant and tunnel portals are wider, as are bridge openings. This means that even if we are building a GWR branch set in 1930 (in standard gauge), these engineering and architectural features would rarely have been moved or altered. It's noticeable that the platform areas around two of the classic GWR branch termini, Moretonhampstead and Ashburton, have roofs and platforms set at broad-gauge distances, though for most of their lives they ran as standard-gauge lines. Thinking about this sort of spacing when planning your layout will quickly give a GWR-influenced feel.

SIGNALLING

The early signals were of a disc and crossbar design and these lasted in some areas until the early 1890s. From the 1860s, semaphore signals were introduced and were subsequently adopted throughout the system. These were a single arm board in a slotted post, with the board dropping into the slot to show 'all clear'. These slotted signals proved unsafe in

Mixed-gauge track, with the outer rails forming the '7ft' and the central rail forming the standard gauge with the rail on the left.

Early GWR disc signal.

Slotted post signal.

some weathers, as the slot could fill with snow or the arm could simply freeze inside it, so the more familiar pivot semaphore was adopted, via a couple of development steps, though usually (opposite to many other railways) working in the lower (9 o'clock to 6 o'clock) quadrant. Distant signal boards were 'notched' with a fishtail shape from 1876 and were subsequently painted yellow to further distinguish them from the red stop boards of other signals after the railway grouping from 1927.

MOTIVE POWER

When looking at the GWR's locomotive development overall, there is much that mirrors the other major railway companies: the standard 0-6-0 goods engines; the 2-6-2 passenger tanks; and up to the large wheel arrangement of the later passenger express engines. The differences, though, are in the detail and at the lower end (which is relevant to our root subject of branch lines). Much of this design was weight and geography dictated. Many of the branch and secondary routes were quite lightly engineered, especially those which the GWR subsequently absorbed, so the company remained with the 'light-weight locomotive' policy through quite a sizeable part of the fleet.

Particularly noticeable, though, was the preference for larger tank engines, as opposed to the other railway companies' gradual shift to tender locomotives. Much of the reasoning for this was the huge traffic from the South Wales coalfields. The lines into the Welsh Valleys were short, had steep gradients and were tightly curved in places. The independent Welsh railway companies that the GWR later absorbed had leant heavily on the 0-6-2 tank engine design and the GWR took this and developed it (and indeed 'Swindon-ized' many of the existing Welsh fleet) with a range of heavy tank engines where the weight of the fuel and water could be kept over a short overall wheelbase, thus maximizing the tractive effort and reducing drag.

The other notable design was in small tank engines for trip freight, shunting and branch work. Without exception, the other British railway companies quickly moved from early designs of 0-4-0 and 0-6-0 saddle tank designs to side tank locomotives for this type of work. The GWR also started with the saddle tanks, but in general terms only shifted to

The last locomotive design. 16XX pannier tank built by British Railways in 1950 to a GWR (Hawksworth) pattern.

Locomotive Superintendents and Chief Mechanical Engineers

Locomotive Superintendents, showing years in the post:
- Daniel Gooch 1837–64
- Joseph Armstrong 1864–77
- William Dean 1877–1902
- George Jackson Churchward 1902–15

Chief Mechanical Engineers (CME):
  (note title change)
- George Jackson Churchward 1915–21
- Charles Collett 1922–41
- Frederick Hawksworth 1941–7.

side tanks for passenger duties, preferring to convert some of the elderly saddles into pannier tanks with flat tops. The standard-gauge saddle tanks began their lives as early as the 1870s and by the early twentieth century the pannier tank revolution was in full swing. Not too many designs of GWR locomotives lasted in regular use from the nineteenth century into the 1930s, but the somewhat iconic pannier tanks were still being built in British Railways days in the 1950s, such was the strength of the basic format. Iconic is not too strong a word, as with Brunel's name being famous, to apply to the pannier tank, which is the one locomotive shape that is recognized by almost anyone as a purely Great Western locomotive. Of course, this may have just as much to do with the Rev. W. Awdry's children's Thomas the Tank Engine stories as anything else, where a pannier tank is the basis for the droll character, 'Duck'.

The first locomotive was delivered to the GWR in January 1838 by the Vulcan Foundry. This, of course, was built to the broad gauge and had a wheel arrangement of 2-2-2, with a set of large driving wheels in the centre flanked by two sets of smaller carrying wheels. This was a style of locomotive still to be used into the twentieth century. The first classes were tender

engines, but this soon developed into a similar tank engine type. With a speed of not much above 30mph (48km/h) and of a lightweight design, they were suitable at the time for any work that was asked of them; they were not branch- or main-line specific. The general development of branch locomotives was more that main-line machines got too fast and too heavy for the branches, not that a specific branch-line locomotive was needed – at least not initially.

One early idea was that of the single vehicle passenger train, the modern version of which is still with us today in the form of the single Diesel Multiple Unit (DMU). The Bristol & Exeter Railway purchased steam rail motors from W.B. Adams of Bow (several line illustrations can be found on the Internet). This vehicle consisted of a long four-wheel carriage with a single-wheeled vertical boiler 'hung' from one end. The ride quality must have been dreadful, but this early GWR acquisition set in place a series of developments of steam rail motors and finally on to the very familiar GWR diesel railcars, which came into being in the mid-twentieth century and lasted until the 1960s, when they were ousted by the pure British Railways versions. This idea of a single unit that did not need to be run around at the terminus was one that the GWR exploited to the full throughout its existence.

CONVERTIBLES

Most of the locomotives built for the GWR in the nineteenth century were constructed to broad gauge, but when it became apparent that this was ending, several classes were built to be 'convertible' – that is, supplied with slender inside frames and axles of 7ft length. These could later be replaced by axles for the standard gauge with relative ease. This was a very forward-looking plan that saved many engines from the scrapyard in 1892 upon the change of gauge. One of these classes was the Armstrong tank, early batches of which were built to broad gauge, while four batches were 'convertible'. It is also at this point that the locomotive styling becomes much closer to what we would regard as a generic-looking twentieth-century steam locomotive, with a flat footplate, long saddle tank and short open cab. The wheels were 4ft 6in (1,372mm) in diameter and it doesn't take much of an imaginative step to see the similarity of this machine to the ubiquitous pannier tank, many of which were initially conversions from these early Armstrong locomotives.

Development through the late nineteenth and early twentieth centuries largely centred on express passenger engines, still mostly with the 2-2-2 wheel arrangement for the top link classes, then into 4-4-0 classes for secondary services. The humble branch lines were mainly forgotten. What rapidly occurred was a programme of stock 'cascading'. Smaller designs that had originally worked city commuter traffic were soon outstripped by traffic weight and were cascaded down to more lowly duties as yard shunters or branch train work. These could include 2-4-0 tender locomotives such as the Barnum class – spritely in their day, but now only suitable for secondary lives – or small fast tank engines such as the

Metro classes. These are usually thought of as branch locomotives, but were originally designed for short urban runs hauling densely loaded four-wheeled coaches. All the main railway companies followed similar strategies: an obvious mirror would be the London, Brighton & South Coast Railway's A1 Terrier class, originally built for fast South London commuter trains, but now largely regarded as a branch locomotive hauling country and coastal traffic. The only nineteenth-century branch-specific engine was the large class designated 517; these were small but powerful machines built to 0-4-2 wheel arrangement with 5ft 2in (1,575mm) driving wheels and a 3ft 8in (1,178mm) trailing pair. There were a multitude of variants within the class, but a 517 is a must if you are looking at an earlier period GWR branch. There are no RTR versions available at the time of writing, but they can be built from a kit or converted from later engines.

7mm scale class 44XX on Crawley MRS's layout.

THE CHURCHWARD AND COLLETT INFLUENCE

It wasn't until George Jackson Churchward took over as Locomotive Superintendent that a medium power, branch-specific passenger locomotive was produced. The two classes, 44XX and 45XX, were out-shopped from 1904 and were immediately successful, especially on West Country routes. For the modeller of the later period a model of the 45XX would be an excellent starting point from which to build a locomotive stud and a 4mm scale model is available from Bachmann.

The last piece in the branch-line jigsaw is the 48XX passenger tank. Designed by Charles Collett and built from 1932, they were produced as two types: 48XX, which were fitted for working with push-pull coaches; and 58XX, which weren't. The confusion is added to as the 48XX were renumbered after World War II in 1946 to make way on the register for the oil-burning 2-8-0s. Thus the 48XX became 14XX, but the 58XX batch remained the same. The result is that the entire double class is known generally as 14XX, even though only half of them carried this class number for just two years before nationalization as British Railways. The 48XX will be dealt with in more detail in a later chapter.

The above few paragraphs on motive power can only give a tiny compressed view into the GWR's branch engine development. The company's class numbers run into the hundreds overall and if this has piqued your interest, then the books by J.H. Russell are worth searching out for more detail. The final consideration is the large number of locomotives that the GWR acquired from other companies, as many of these were suitable for branch-line work.

Ian Smith's stunning recreation of an early GWR scene in 2mm finescale.

THE 1923 GROUPING

During World War I, all British railway companies were taken into Government hands. As a result, it was soon discovered that attempting to move goods and munitions around effectively was a complete headache, as each of the private companies (more than 100 of them) ran differing operating procedures and paperwork systems. Therefore, instead of making the operation easier, it only highlighted the difficulties of operating a whole-country rail system with one common aim. After the war, it was decided that the system should be streamlined by sectioning the British railways system into four defined areas. All the companies within an area would be combined into one group, giving the Government more control over the situation, in that it would only have to deal with four tightly controlled systems.

The four new companies would still have a degree of autonomy, but be overseen by a Government body. Thus the Southern Railway controlled the trackage in the south-east and a little of the West Country; the London & North Eastern Railway (LNER) covered the east of England and east coast of Scotland; and the London, Midland & Scottish Railway (LMS) held the Midlands and west of Scotland. But what of the area to the west? Why, the Great Western Railway of course. The company already controlled large swathes of the West Midlands and East Wales, the area around the Bristol Channel and much of Devon and Cornwall. It had bought or operated many of the smaller lines in the area already, so it was really just of a case of sweeping up the Cambrian Railways in West Wales and the smaller companies around the South Wales coalfields, while retaining the company name.

You will note several things from the absorbed railways list. Firstly, it gave the GWR a virtual monopoly over the South Wales coalfield; secondly, assumption of the Cambrian Railways (the plural in the title giving an indication of that company's ferocious takeover of many other minor lines) gave the GWR control over almost all of western Wales. This would have been the feather in the cap for the GWR, as even though the money was in the coal in the south, the addition of the Cambrian meant that on a pure public relations angle, the GWR could colour the railway map chocolate brown from the Midlands right through to the western coast of the British Isles – now the title Great Western really did mean Great Western.

The third and less obvious factor for our purposes was that the GWR now had ownership of even more of the minor branch byways, including some built under the Light Railway Act similar to the Culm Valley. For the GWR modeller who is slightly short of space these lines are a gift, as the full might of the GWR is coupled with the more quirky and compact railway stations. Lastly, the list above also quietly contains three true narrow-gauge railways: the Corris Railway; the Welshpool & Llanfair Railway; and the Vale of Reidol Railway. At 2ft 3in (686mm), 2ft 6in (762mm) and 1ft 11.5in (597mm) gauges respectively, they were hardly GWR Swindon standard, but they once again give the GWR modeller another option.

Railways Grouped into the GWR in 1923

- Alexandra Docks
- Barry Railway
- Brecon & Merthyr Railway
- Burry Port & Gwendreath Valley Railway
- Cambrian Railways
- Cardiff Railway
- Cleobury Mortimer & Ditton Priors Light Railway
- Llanelli & Mynydd Mawr Railway
- Midland & South Western Junction Railway
- Neath & Brecon Railway
- Port Talbot Railway
- Rhonda & Swansea Bay Railway
- Rhymney Railway
- South Wales Mineral Railway
- Swansea Harbour Trust
- Taff Vale Railway.

Great Western narrow gauge – the absorbed (via the Cambrian Railways) Vale of Rheidol line at Devil's Bridge station.

THE INTERWAR YEARS' POPULAR BRANCH-LINE PERIOD

The period from the Grouping in 1923 to the outbreak of war in 1939 would be regarded by most as the classic period of any British railway company and none more so than the GWR. In part this is true: the railway became more glamorous, faster, built larger and more powerful locomotives and developed what some regard as a standard style. The previous section on the 1923 Grouping proves that the company was far from standard with its mix of constituent lines, but the public face was important and, like the other Grouping companies, the GWR took full advantage of the advertising and publicly machines of the day to encourage the travelling public to use it. And the financial reality was that passengers were what it needed most.

Almost as soon as the GWR had gained control of the Welsh coalfields due to the Grouping, the market in coal began to drop. The GWR had quickly scrapped much of the absorbed company's locomotive studs and rolling stock, only keeping what was considered to be useful long term. But in order to move this new traffic, it had to increase its own motive power by designing new or updated classes to suit. The other more general downturn was the fall in freight traffic across the entire British system. This was compounded at a local level by a new breed of military-service trained drivers coming on to the roads after World War I, coupled with the availability of cheap ex-War Department vehicles for them to purchase with which to start their own delivery companies and bus companies – all this in direct competition with the railway. This led the GWR to increase its own local road delivery services and to begin a bidding war to take over the local bus operators. The main problem was that the GWR, like the other three of the 'Big Four', was considered a 'common carrier'. This meant that by law it had to take whatever traffic it was offered and furthermore was obliged to publish the carriage rates up front. This left it completely unarmed to fight any undercutting from independent road hauliers.

By the 1930s, this competition problem was starting to bite and more secondary and branch mileage was closed during the years 1929–32 than during the 1960s. The GWR had one option – to present itself as the holidaymakers' route to a dream with its unparalleled access to the coastline of the West Country and West and North Wales. The GWR's direction was now to create the best, most glamorous and fastest trains to get them there. In some ways, this was a boom time for the GWR's seaside branches, with more freedom of movement allowed to the general public and before the rise of private car ownership. It was far less the case for the inland lines, with only declining local passenger traffic and high competition for local goods carriage.

WORLD WAR II AND THE END OF THE GWR

At the outbreak of war in 1939 Britain's railways were once more taken into Government hands. The glamour days of the super-fast express races in the 1930s were now over and a period of knuckling down for the war effort soon began. This was a low point for the British railway system in general; the four Grouping companies went into the war after the trade slump of the 1930s and were now literally hammered both in work terms and through enemy bombardment. The GWR came off slightly lighter than others with regard to the latter, although it incurred great damage in the Midlands and its port areas. The demand for industry in the Midlands to build munitions meant that it took a large amount of the strain in moving materials and coal for the entire period of the conflict.

POST-WORLD WAR II

During the war years, any new technical locomotive and rolling-stock development was largely curtailed and it was not until after the war that the GWR's last CME, Frederick Hawksworth, resumed with new designs, notably three new pannier tanks for shunting (94XX and 15XX) and light branch work (16XX, pictured earlier). Thus the GWR's locomotive fleet went

Tip

For the modeller, these immediate post-war years are an underdone, but rich period – the stock still holds the GWR character, but a wartime landscape can be built around it, with physical damage and evidence of defence such as sandbags, tank traps and the like very much to the fore. Tiny touches such as painting platform canopy supports with black and white stripes and painting the platform edges white, both measures which came about through World War II blackout regulations, will help plant the period firmly in the 1945–8 timeframe. Troops would still be very much in evidence and the population as a whole would be on the move, returning to rebuild their lives. The downside is that it is a very poorly photographed period, although there is a stream of general shots and film footage from the mainstream news agencies that can be of great help in this respect, with much of it now available on the Internet.

out with a bit of a whimper of small unmemorable engines, for the writing for the four 1923 Grouping companies was certainly now on the wall.

The 1923 Grouping of the railways into four companies had really only been a lightly veiled precursor to nationalization. Government control in World War I had exposed the inefficiencies of a multiple company rail system and now after this had happened again only twenty-one years later, it was decided that this type of Government railway organization should be long term. Not only was this regarded as expedient on a national security level, but the political landscape had changed to a more Socialist model, in which Government control of industry was seen as the way forward – the 'Big Four' Grouping companies would be nationalized into one large state-run British Railways. There was a brief swansong of the GWR, when war-weary locomotives resumed their 1930s workload, albeit in dull worn-out livery and with tired and battered rolling stock. Little was done in any form until the blaze of the new British Railways corporate identity was thrust upon it.

THE GWR UNDER BRITISH RAILWAYS

Nationalization in 1948 did not stop everything dead. The GWR's maintenance shops still carried on much as in earlier times and although new British Railways rolling-stock designs quickly appeared, much of the locomotive fleet still continued as before. The Western's traditions were still maintained and even GWR-designed locos were still newly constructed, the very last being a Hawksworth-designed 16XX pannier in 1955, a full seven years after the GWR ceased to exist as a nominally private company. Also in this year the 'modernization plan' began and the idea of a steam railway system covering the British Isles was tipped into the box marked 'old ways'. Although the GWR's locomotive shops turned to building British Railways 'standard' steam locomotive designs, diesel and electric would be the future. The new world was clean, bright and shiny and there was no public appetite for green locomotives with copper-capped chimneys pulling chocolate and cream coaches down lush green leafy byways. Or was there?

CHAPTER THREE

GOODS TRAFFIC

GENERAL GWR GOODS TRAFFIC HISTORY

By the time that it had consolidated, the GWR could boast a vast fleet of goods vehicles: some 60,000 at the end of the nineteenth century, rising to just short of 90,000 by the 1920s. The World War I Government had introduced a country-wide pooling system for all railway company wagons. Prior to that, each vehicle had to be returned to its home system; usually in an empty state within five days or the receiving railway company would be issued with a fine. Pooling meant that the wagon could either be worked onward with a new load, or worked back to the parent company in a full condition. This mutually agreeable wagon pooling system was regarded as a success and was extended after the war – first with regard to open wagons, then extending to vans, though there were a large number of other vehicles that were not included in this and which used the previous non-pool immediate return arrangement.

A parallel development also existed in the standardization of many wagon parts under the auspices of the Railway Clearing House (RCH), meaning that a vehicle that was damaged could be repaired en route or at the destination by the host company without having to be returned home as a 'cripple'. This generally disadvantaged the GWR, as more wagons travelled on to it than away, meaning that it repaired more foreign wagons than those of its own being repaired elsewhere. Both of these systems smoothed the way that goods traffic was handled and continued into the British Railways era after 1948, when further standardization took place.

As mentioned earlier, the initial reason behind the original GWR company was to transfer not only westward travelling passengers from London,

but also to speed the highly lucrative port traffic in and out of Bristol. It is difficult to visualize from the standpoint of the twenty-first century just how much freight was carried on Britain's rail network before World War I, when the road network was still under-developed and quite poorly maintained. Essentially everything except the most local traffic was carried by rail and, as explained in the previous chapter, the railways were legally required to do so until well into the nationalization years under the term 'common carrier'.

As an aside: it is usually assumed that the branch-line system was deliberately dismantled during the 1960s as part of the modernization plan and under pressure from the road lobby, but while this is partially true, it was also a continuation of the rise in local road haulage post-1918.

JUST OPENS AND VANS

Like the LMS and the LNER, the GWR owned a large number of specialist goods vehicles – from manure wagons (to service the large number of railway company stables), to those with a unique triangular frame to carry aircraft propellers. Most numerous, though, were the simple box vans and open merchandise wagons, the latter outnumbering anything else in the fleet. For the branch-line modeller, it is these two groups which are the most logical to study, as the majority of general goods traffic (around 90 per cent) was carried in opens (often covered with a canvas sheet) and vans. Although some of the more specialist vehicles did appear on the smaller branch lines, it was more often than not due to a specific dedicated traffic, for example milk tank wagons serving a dairy. It is the study of these vans and opens and the sub-

Vacuum-fitted MINK van stands at Didcot. Note the axle tie bar and Dean/Churchward brakes.

sequent modelling that will give that elusive correct feel. It is important to bear in mind that including too many specialist vehicles on a model layout will work against the dull and workaday feel of most branches.

The problem for the modeller sitting in the comfort of the twenty-first century is that photographs of pre-1940s goods trains fall a poor second behind the glamour of the passenger express, and the branch goods train is quite a way behind that. If you could afford a camera back then, you were unlikely to expend film on a grubby little branch pick-up goods train. The result is that researching the branch goods is a bit of a hit and miss exercise. The post-1940s period is slightly better served photographically, though, as stated earlier, wagon design had moved

on, so although these photos do give some slight indication of wagon flows, the actual vehicle types will likely be different to those used during the GWR period. The danger for the modeller (and particularly the novice) is that this leads to a tendency to copy other people's models. This may in some instances be very accurate; however, what usually happens is that mistakes and assumptions get replicated. On the other hand, sometimes assumptions are all that we have to go on.

One final consideration is the pre-1940s use of private owner wagons (strictly speaking referred to as 'owner wagons'; the 'private' prefix is a model railway term). As well as its own and foreign company wagons, the GWR handled a colossal number of

Tip
Build up a collection of branch goods train photos and analyse the make-up of each train. This information can be used to depict accurately similar good trains on your layout. The warning once again is that photographers would have been drawn to the unusual, not the humdrum, so a little pinch of salt needs to be taken if there are large numbers of specialist wagons in the photos, unless there is corroborating evidence to suggest that this was in any way normal. There are several photos of entire farms being moved, both machinery and livestock all on one train. These photos were most probably taken due to the unusual circumstance and not because this was something which happened on the branch each week. This sort of train is useful to the modeller as an occasional 'special', but is easy to overdo.

owner wagons, many of which emanated from the coalfields of South Wales. These were counted in the thousands and any period photo of a colliery pithead often shows long lines of identically lettered wagons waiting to be loaded from the screens, or full wagons ready for dispatch. Note that in nearly all cases the wagons would have this identical owner-ship lettering. The modeller is naturally dawn to the endless RTR colourful liveries that are produced, but a single-track railway line with a colliery at the end would probably only see a few (or maybe only one) livery of colliery-owned wagon throughout its exist-ence. The exception would be wagons owned and lettered for a local coal trader within your model's locality. These owner wagons, like the specialist GWR wagons, should be treated with some caution on a small branch layout.

MODELLING THE GREAT WESTERN'S GOODS STOCK

PROJECT ONE: SIMPLE OPEN WAGON KIT

The natural and obvious place for the novice to begin is by buying a few RTR wagons. This may or may not be a good idea – it really depends how serious, or how accurate, you wish to be. Most of the newer crop of models are very good, but the further back the production runs are, the less realistic and toy-like they become, so some weeding out and a degree of thought is needed. Many of the older models are built on a standard model chassis unit, so liberties are taken with the bodies, resulting in them being stretched or compressed to fit. Depending on how fussy you are about accuracy, it's worth giving these a careful assessment before you buy. Do not assume that because it is a commercially available product, that all is correct.

Once you have built up a small selection of RTR wagons, the first upward step is to augment those with a few plastic kits. The plastic wagon kit has been around since the late 1950s and the quality of the current offerings is generally very high. There are, though, a few modifications and improvements that can be made to even the simplest kit.

KIT BUILDING

At one time, kit building was seen as something that was slightly specialist. This idea has gradually faded away, but since a couple of generations have grown up during a time when Airfix kits were not the con-structional toy of choice, many novice modellers are wary of dipping a toe in the water. This is unfortunate, as not only is there a lot of modelling pleasure to be gained, but kits can fill in many of the gaps that the RTR market does not provide for. There used to be a steep cost differential that made some kits look unattractive as a purchase, but in recent times the RTR prices have increased considerably (albeit along with the quality), so now the relative cost of trying a few kits is far from prohibitive. In fact, at the time of writing this differential has widened still further,

O29 open wagon. Disc wheels, double-sided Morton brakes.

making a lot of the kits far cheaper than most RTR wagons of a similar type, even if a few extra parts might need to be added to the cost.

The subject for this first project is a long-lived kit from the Ratio Models range. This kit has been around for many years, but has been marginally upgraded and now includes metal wheels and axle bearings as standard. It is also distributed to the model trade by the trackwork producer Peco, so is freely available from most model shops that carry the Peco range.

Materials required:
• Ratio Models GWR open wagon kit, Ref: 564
• Plastic strip 20 × 40thou (Slater's or Evergreen)
• Plastic rod 1mm diameter (Slater's or Evergreen)
• Blu-tack

• All-purpose adhesive such as UHU
• Liquid plastic solvent such as Mek-Pak and small a non-plastic brush with which to apply it
• Paint.

Tools required:
• Cutting mat or similar work surface
• Sanding stick or needle files
• 2mm and 1mm drill bits
• Craft knife or scalpel
• Brushes.

This might at first glance seem like a long list of things to buy, but all of the tools will be used for future projects in the book, as will the several shades of Humbrol acrylic paint which will be listed later.

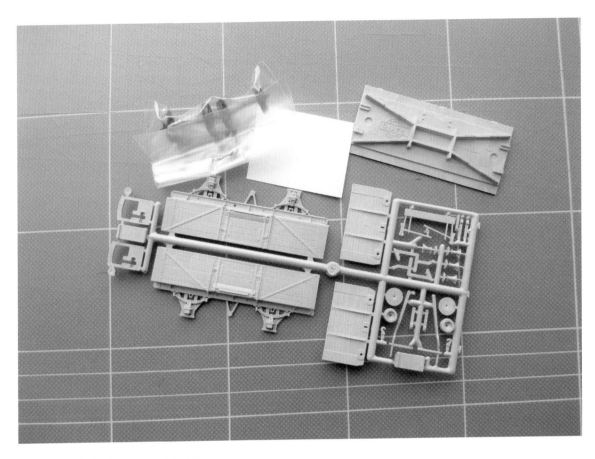

Contents of the Ratio Models kit.

EVALUATING THE KIT

Don't just charge into building a kit. Take a good look at all the parts first and get a feel for how things go together. The instructions should be read through as well, even though in a lot of cases they may not quite match the quality of the kit.

The Ratio Models kit pictured here is more or less complete except for paint and adhesive, which is one reason why it was chosen as a first project. It does differ from many similar kits in that the solebar/axle boxes are in one piece along with the body sides. Most similar kits would separate these. This does cause a small problem which will be dealt with as we go through the build, but first a little history.

DIAGRAM O29 OPEN WAGON

The wagon represented by the Ratio kit is based on a Diagram O29 wagon built in 1933. The O29 was an intermediate design, having no sheet rail (a U-shaped bar that could be raised to lift a tarpaulin sheet off the load and let the rain run off). These sheet rails were beloved by the GWR, but disliked by the other rail companies, so the GWR begrudgingly discontinued them. The wagon was also one of the last to feature a 9ft (2,743mm) long wheelbase before the shift to a preferred 10ft (3,048mm) length. There were Morton brake handles fitted on both sides, as per the then current RCH rules (thus the shunters could avoid the dangerous practice of ducking under a wagon to reach the brake handle), but the actual brakes were only fitted to one side. The wagons were very long-lived, lasting into British Railways days and there are a couple of examples which have been preserved should you wish to examine one further.

CLEANING UP AND ADJUSTING

Firstly, the axle-box problem needs to be attended to. The kit was originally designed for plastic wheel sets with relatively long stub axles. It now comes supplied with standard 26mm long metal axles and brass bearing cups. If these are pushed all the way into the holes and the wagon is assembled correctly with regard to the body parts, then, quite simply –

the wheels will fall out; so a little trickery is required. First, open the axle-box holes out to 2mm using a 2mm drill bit as shown, held between the finger and thumb and rotated gently. Do this before taking any parts off the sprue.

Clean up the area, then add the bearings into a 'puddle' of all-purpose adhesive so that the bearings sit proud of the axle box by around 1mm as shown.

The axle boxes are opened out with a 2mm drill.

Axle bearings 'float' in a puddle of all-purpose adhesive and stand about 1mm proud of the plastic moulding.

Notches are filed in the solebars with a needle file.

It is safer to take a drop of glue to the part using a cocktail stick or a match, rather than straight from the tube. Let this all dry completely, then remove the part from the sprue, clean it up and remove any flash. ('Flash' is the term used for any excess plastic around a particular part.)

The other connected issue is to get the corners of the sides and ends to match correctly. This isn't helped by a slightly over-length solebar. To correct this, first clean off any flash, then 'saw' two small notches into the ends using a flat needle file, as shown by the knife point in the photo. This allows the solebar to drop into the recess at the back of the buffer beam and create a nice snug fit. Don't worry if you take off a little too much; it is far easier to fill this afterwards than to try to correct a glaringly obvious mismatched body corner joint.

BODY

Now remove and clean up the ends and open up the buffer stock holes with a 1mm drill bit in a similar fashion to the axle boxes. When all parts are clean and tidy, you can trial-fit the whole lot with the wheel sets. This is a real juggling exercise and you may find that using some Blu-tack to fix the parts in place will be a great help. The wheels should sit parallel and be a snug fit between the bearings. Adjust these if need be and make sure that the corners all meet at 45 degrees with no gaps. Any mistakes here will be glaringly obvious. The trial set-up should look like the photos shown on the opposite page.

When you are entirely happy, start to stick the sides and ends together using liquid solvent applied with a brush. The use of a small engineer's square is useful, but not critical. The printed lines on your cutting mat will work just as well. Add the ends to one side and let things dry thoroughly. The solvent has a habit of pulling the ends inward, so keep checking that all is square as the joints 'go off'. Finally, add the second side, trapping the wheels inside as you fix.

Add the floor from above. This may be a little tight fitting, so sand the edges gently using a sanding stick until the fit is good. Before you stick, make sure that the assembled wagon (without the floor) will run through a point and that it will stand on a dead flat

Dry run of the assembly. Make sure that all corner joints line up and wheels are trapped firmly.

Final assembly. Make sure that all corners are square before adding liquid solvent.

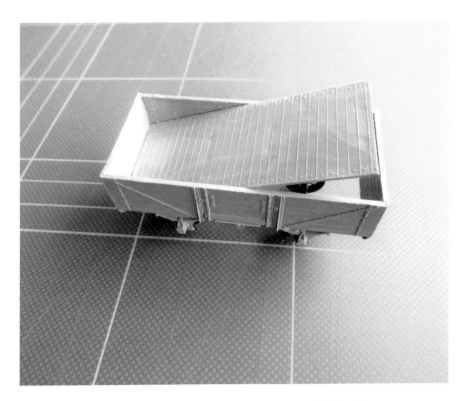

The floor drops in from the top and will need fettling to fit.

surface, such as a piece of glass, with all four wheels in contact. If not, 'twist gently' until all is well, then add the floor and attach it by running brush-fulls of solvent around the inside edges.

BRAKES, CORNER PLATES AND BUFFERS

Add the single set of brake gear between the wheels. This may need sanding slightly where it joins the floor and on the brake shoes themselves to get a good position that lines up with the tyres, but does not rub on them. Add the brake lever, noting that the 'cam' is unusually on the same side as the brake gear in this case. You may need to flex the brake lever slightly. This can be done by warming it in warm water or rubbing it between the fingers for a while. Don't be alarmed if it snaps. This happens to everyone. Just take a deep breath, stick the bits together and start again.

One area where a simple wagon can fall down is the corner plates. On the model they are seen as part of the side or end, but of course prototypi-cally they are angled steel plates that wrap around

The lever with the cam is fitted on the same side as the brake gear.

Corner plates should be gently rounded.

Make sure that buffers are straight and with the ribs in the correct position.

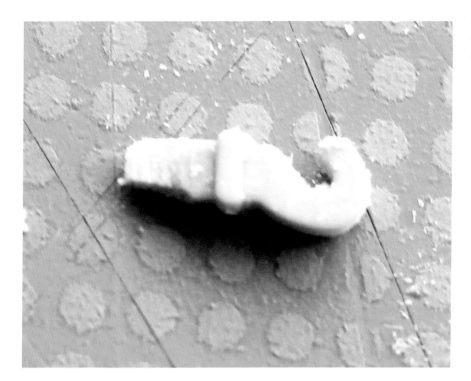

The coupling hooks need to be thinned to fit.

the corners to stop the sides and ends collapsing outward. In order to make them look like one piece, gently sand with a sanding stick from both sides in a curving motion, rounding the corners in the process. Adding a little solvent and allowing it to dry halfway through this process can help.

The buffers can now be added after they have been cleaned up, noting the position of the ribs on the shanks.

If you intend using one of the commercial auto-coupling units, the plastic coupling hook included in the kit can be fitted now. The whole part can be thinned a little, but the shaft needs to be quite severely reduced to fit. This is far easier than trying to make the hole in the buffer beam larger.

BRAKE RODDING

One part that is not included in the kit is the rod connecting the single brake lever to the side with the brake. Cut a length of 1mm plastic rod to a shade over-length and then trial-fit, removing a little off the end until it is an interference fit without bowing. Then add a drop of solvent to fix in place. Finally, the

door bangers can be added to the solebar in line with the plates on the doors. These are quite fragile and may break, but can be easily replaced with a short length of 20 × 40thou plastic strip.

PAINTING AND FINISHING

This wagon is perfect for the most common GWR modelling period of the 1930s, but it would have been relatively new at that time, so the finish in most cases needs to be 'grubby ex-works' rather than decrepit. Start with giving the entire body a light coat of Humbrol Dark Earth (29). The underframe can be given an equally light coat of Humbrol Red Leather (62). The corner plates can receive a touch of this as well. Let this initial coat dry thoroughly before proceeding any further.

Then give the outer areas an all-over light coat of Tank Grey (67). Don't try to cover the areas thoroughly; rather, let the base colours bleed through a little, indicating some wear and tear. Unless you are modelling a post-war period these wagons would still be newish, probably in fairly good condition and would not have any replacement planks as yet. The wagon grey colour can be variable, as many of the

A length of 1mm plastic rod is added between the V hangers.

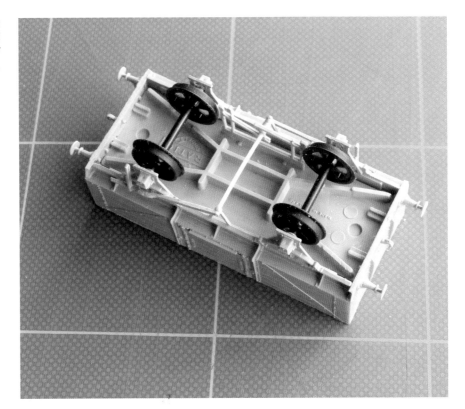

A base coat of Earth Brown is applied to the bodywork inside and out.

Tip

Keep the area where the transfer is to be placed fairly wet. This will allow you to slide the transfer around until correctly positioned. Then draw the excess water away with a tissue.

The transfer backing sheet is slid away, leaving the transfer on the wet surface where it can be adjusted.

photos show. Not only would each paint shop mix their own shade, but the sun would have a bleaching effect, meaning that the 'standard' wagon grey could be anything from almost black through to a quite pale sea grey.

The interior of the wagon can be dealt with by first using a wash of a cream colour to represent new wood, allowing this to dry, then a final thin wash of Tank Grey or black to highlight the planking. The paint should be allowed to dry thoroughly, preferably for twenty-four hours before adding the transfers enclosed with the kit.

The transfers should be applied as per the kit instructions by soaking each individual part in a saucer of water and applying to the wagon surface.

Any item of rolling stock benefits from a very thin coat of varnish (Humbrol 49). This helps to seal the paint and fix the transfers – waterslide transfers have a habit of drying and flaking with handling if this is not done. Any final light weathering can now be carried out, such as a little rust or dirt applied to the underframe and buffers.

The basic open merchandise wagon was an exceptionally numerous vehicle and even the smallest of GWR branch-line layouts would need at least three

The completed Ratio O29 open wagon.

of these. Other opens wagons suitable for the later periods are available in 4mm scale from Parkside Models, but for earlier periods the Coopercraft Models kits are a good place to start and are similar in build techniques to this one. Further to that would be some of the smaller kit manufacturers who produce white-metal and brass kits for the earlier historical periods. However, if you feel that modelling in metal is a bit of a jump, a layout full of the Ratio plastic kits such as this will certainly be more than acceptable for a post-1930 setting.

GWR GOODS BRAKE VANS

Once you have a wagon or two you will need a brake van. There are several kits on the market in 4mm and 7mm scales as well as basic RTR offerings in 4mm and 2mm scales.

The GWR did not build any of its own standard-gauge brake vans until 1871, though it had acquired a few from other companies along the way as a result of its mergers and takeovers. These were in the main wooden, outside-framed and quite a mixture of styles. The first GWR brakes were, as you may expect, built with a single end veranda, though not quite as may be assumed. One of the urban myths that has built up (again mainly through the modelling press) is that there is a standard GWR brake van similar to the one pictured here. In fact, as you are rapidly finding out, there is not a GWR standard anything.

The early vans in both standard and broad gauges were made of wood, had a short wheelbase of around 9ft (2,743mm) in size, and the veranda was completely lacking a roof of any kind. This soon changed, as a roof was added and there were many variations on this general theme until the end of the nineteenth century.

TOAD brake van with immaculate paintwork and late 1930s lettering style stands at Didcot Railway Centre.

Withdrawal of these early vans started in the 1880s, but newer versions that were longer and heavier were built into the World War I years. It wasn't until the late 1880s that the first nod toward what we think of as the standard type began, with an experiment in materials and a shift to vans being partly constructed from metal sheeting. The result was a 20ft long (6,096mm) van with a 13ft (3,962mm) wheelbase and a single covered veranda. This was the first van to adopt the 'AA' diagram prefix common to all future brake vans, becoming AA3/TOAD (there will be more on the diagrams and naming later in this chapter).

There then followed several decades of development on this basic design. The weight was increased, a six-wheel version was introduced and several non-standard body designs were built, including road vans (with a pair of doors in the side) and the fully enclosed Severn Tunnel vans.

In 1912, a stretched AA3 was produced (AA11), giving a van of 24ft long (7,315mm) with a 16ft wheelbase (4,877mm). At this point, we have now reached the TOAD brake that we all know and love. Many slight variants of this design were built, but it visually stayed the same until the end of the GWR, the last

being built under the nationalized British Railways in 1949. However, there were still upgraded wooden vans lurking on the system into the 1940s, so anything is possible. Not likely, but possible nonetheless.

This short history is again only a tiny snapshot of the development history, as the GWR's vans were many and highly varied, but don't necessarily relate to our branch-line subject.

Tip

Two vans do warrant a special mention – aside from the shorter early wooden vans, the GWR-built vans, designated AA7, for its Metropolitan lines and for trains serving Smithfield Market. These two are outwardly similar and for our purposes are usefully short at 16ft length – a saving of 25mm in 4mm scale model terms. Although they have only been available in kit and conversion form, they may be just the job for the space staved GWR modeller.

PRACTICALITIES

If you have a wagon, then you need a brake van to go behind it. Brake (originally 'break') vans are essentially the riding position for the guard, who is the eyes of the driver at the rear of the train. His basic job is to stop the rear portion if the train 'breaks', to slow a loose-coupled train on a steep downgrade and to warn any train travelling behind if his train makes an unscheduled stop for any reason, by laying detonators on the rails behind and planting flags as a warning. This basic safety requirement still holds true today and is the reason for many people's reluctance to accept driver-only trains. The brake van and guard are also a requirement if the train is making an awkward reversing movement, where once again the guard (now at the front) becomes the eyes of the driver and can communicate to him using flags and whistles. Again, to some extent there are still manoeuvres that would require this sort of operation today.

The following project is a straightforward upgrade of a basic and ubiquitous Hornby RTR model of a later build GWR brake van.

TOAD brake van stands at Horsted Keynes. This is a working van and the condition represents how most vans would have appeared.

PROJECT TWO: AA20 GOODS BRAKE VAN

Materials required:
• Hornby GWR brake van
• Guard
• Lamps – Springside or similar
• All-purpose adhesive
• Acrylic paint.

Tools required:
• Sanding stick
• Flat needle file
• Brushes.

APPRAISING THE MODEL

The Hornby brake van is a freely available model which has its root in an Airfix product from thirty-five years ago. The chassis has been changed very slightly over the years, but the body section remains largely as designed. Is it worth using though?

The number printed on it suggests that it is one of the first batch of Diagram AA20 vans built in 1934. A quick run over the chassis with a ruler shows that it is the correct 24ft long with a 16ft wheelbase – so far, so good. In common with most RTR models, the whole chassis is a little on the chunky side. Other downsides are the mould lines on the buffers and buffer beam, and the brakes which are in front of, and not in line with, the wheels. Luckily the footsteps tend to hide this. Normally one of the first things to look at would be to upgrade the brakes visually, but to be honest it would be tricky and more trouble than it's worth – you would be better off using a kit brake van instead.

The body is good. The only obvious defect for an AA20 van are the two-pane windows, as single-pane windows were fitted to all GWR brake vans after Diagram AA15.

The Hornby (ex-Airfix) brake, straight out of the box, showing mould lines and a very clean livery.

CHASSIS

First, separate the body from the chassis – this should just pull apart. Remove the couplings, which on this model just pulled off. Then, using a sanding stick or needle file, clean the mould lines off the buffer faces and the buffer beam. Clean any loose bits away and paint the whole visible chassis with a coat of Humbrol Tank Grey (67) with a drop of black (33) mixed in to darken it to match the body. This takes the shine off the slippery engineering plastic used for the chassis moulding. Finally, touch in the buffer heads and axle springs with a little Leather (62) colour. This can also be lightly drifted on to the solebars, but don't overdo it.

BODY

Paint the inside of the veranda roof with Tamiya XF-2 White. This may need several coats to cover the dark grey. This is not visible from most viewing angles, but you'll know it's there and it does reflect light into the veranda. Don't try to remove the roof to work on the model. It is very firmly fixed and the chances of irreparably breaking it are very high.

Mould lines removed from the chassis unit.

The veranda roof should be painted white.

Next comes the most delicate operation of the project. The superfluous window bars have to be removed. The pair on the veranda are awkward, to say the least. Carefully make two 'saw' cuts in one of them using the serrated edge of a flat needed file; not too close to the edge. Then carefully clean the inside edges of the opening. Take special care not to catch the file on the veranda supports. Then repeat the process with the other three. Because of the roof being stuck, it is near impossible to glaze the windows from the inside as would be usual, but a liquid glazing product such as Kristal Kleer may be used.

Sawing the window bar with a needle file.

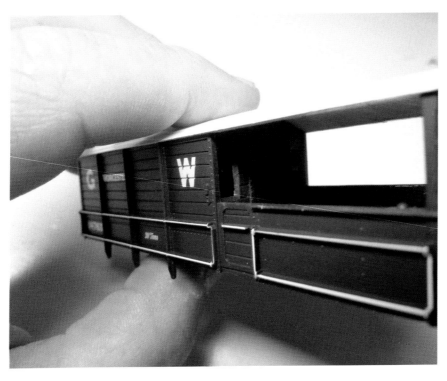

The completed window surgery.

TOP COATS

The van can now be reassembled. The rest of the work is mostly painting. Firstly, the roof can be given a few thin coats of Light Grey (64). The van roofs were originally out-shopped with lead white paint, but with a constant atmosphere of chimney smuts, rain and coal dust blown from loco tenders and coal wagons, these would rapidly darken.

When the roof is thoroughly dry, the ends and sides can be given a wash of Tank Grey. Work with the van upside down so that the pigment settles under features and the roof line rather than at the bottom.

Before this is totally dry, dry-brush a coat of Light Grey (64) on to the entire van, really working the pigment into the surface. This should bring the colour of the van down and give it a dusty feel. Working the grey into the lettering gives a worn, flaky impression.

Washes and Dry-Brushing

Washes can be achieved by adding paint to the very tip of the brush, then dipping quickly into water, giving a 30/70 mix of dilute paint. This can be drawn down the model (usually working with the model held upside down) and pulling any excess paint mix off with a brush that has been wiped dry. Practise this on a cheap or old model first. A larger brush works best (No. 2 or 3), as it will carry more paint mix and you will be able to work quickly over the model's surface.

Dry-brushing is the exact opposite. Take a small amount of paint on to the brush, wiping most of it off again. Then scrub the surface of the model to force the remaining pigment into the surface. Alternatively, wipe the brush over the surface to pick out any detail, such as a line of rivets. Again, practise this technique on something less valuable first. Keep an old worn-out brush for this process. Do not use a brand-new one, as this action will ruin it in seconds.

BELOW: *A light wash of Tank Grey starts to blend the van into a single unit.*

Dry-brushing Light Grey into the surface.

DETAILS

Finally, a few details can be added. The brake handle on the veranda can be painted white, a guard figure can be added (here a Dapol figure was used with his feet cut off to reduce his height) and lamps can be added at the end and sides. Photographs show that some vans had ladders strapped to the footsteps, particularly if they were departmental or pure branch vans, though this is highly optional.

This should give you a van which looks as if it has had some steady service. Painting dates were not very frequent for brake vans, so this slightly tatty, but not derelict feel is entirely typical.

The Hornby/Airfix van is cheap and readily available either new, or it can be picked up second-hand and unboxed for as little as £5.00 at model shows. So as a first try for this sort of conversion it's hard to beat. At the time of writing, Hornby has announced a replacement model of an AA15 van which will be far superior, but of course less fun to alter.

TELEGRAPHIC CODES AND BUILD DIAGRAMS

The GWR, like other rail companies, used telegraph messages to transmit details of stock movements and other operational orders. To save time and space, much of this was transmitted by using a specific one-word code for each type of item. Although they covered all of the railway's operational activity, the most well-known usage was that of identifying wagons or groups of wagons. This was used to advantage to calculate both train length and stock availability. Much of this expansive list of coding is available online … and it is very expansive. What concerns us here is the names that were used for the most likely and numerous wagon, as they are often still referred to by these code names.

Many wagons used names from the animal kingdom; this gave an endless choice and made the names distinctive and therefore less likely to confuse, as opposed to a code such as A1, A2, A3 and so on, though some related directly to the actual vehicle type. Thus the code for the numerous open wagons as dealt with in Project One is simply 'OPEN', whereas the equally common series of closed vans are coded 'MINK'. As stated earlier, special wagons were not overly common on branch lines, so below is a selection of some of the more likely and ubiquitous types:

• OPEN – open wagon without sheet rail
• OPEN A – with sheet rail

The completed Hornby TOAD brake van.

- MINK – van
- MEX – cattle wagon
- MACAW – timber bolster wagon
- SERPENT – agricultural machinery wagon
- TOAD – brake van
- BEETLE – passenger train rated cattle wagon
- FRUIT – passenger train rated fruit van
- CORDON – gas tank wagon; often used to deliver gas for rural station lighting.

Just to add to what is already a confusing system – in 1943, when under wartime Government control, some of the names were changed to tie in with other company's systems in order to create a country-wide coding. For example, 'OPEN' became 'HIGH'. The above list should cover most of the wagon groups that a branch-line layout would need and you will note from the first that there was often a lettered sub-class coding to differentiate certain wagon characteristics, such as if they were fitted with vacuum brakes. This coding system partly remains today under Network Rail, notably with the departmental wagons that use water-linked names, such as 'MERMAID', 'WALRUS' and so on.

DIAGRAM NUMBERS

You will have noticed from the first two projects that the vehicle is often denoted using a diagram number. This was the number of the drawing sheet used to build the vehicle and was also coded by using an initial single or double capital letter. The open wagon using O (O29) and the brake AA (AA20). Again, confusingly, although they run date-numerically there is often overlap – diagram 12 may still be being built after diagram 13 has finished. Diagram 12 may be a large class and so will run on, whereas 13 may be a single vehicle with a small specific modification.

There are also what look like oddities: G diagrams start with well wagons, then shift to 'motor car vans', which looks odd at first glance, until you spot that both carry road vehicles even though they are entirely different shapes. The list below gives a few likely examples.

- O – open wagons
- V – vans
- R – manure wagons
- Y – passenger train rated fruit vans
- Z – gunpowder vans
- W – cattle wagons
- H – flat wagons.

CHAPTER FOUR

COACHING STOCK

GENERAL CONSIDERATIONS

The model trade is fairly generous when it comes to RTR coaching stock, though there is always a rumour that not much of it gets sold compared to the more desirable locomotives and the cheaper wagon models. In 7mm scale, there are a multitude of suitable branch-line stock kits in plastic and brass; Slater's produces a range of beautiful coach kits in plastic that are a very good starting point. In OO and N, there is an almost parallel selection of RTR models. Where this can fall down for the branch-line modeller is that these are pretty deliberately aimed at the GWR's later periods (late 1930s and post-war). This is a manufacturing/sales efficiency issue – a late-period coach can be produced in both GWR and in early

Clerestory coach showing end-frame detail and window reveal paint colours.

BR liveries, thus making the production costs more efficient for the manufacturer and resulting in bigger sales. The net result is that layouts in OO and N become identikit copies with the compulsory B-set pair and an Autocoach (in 4mm scale both Hornby, ex-Airfix/Dapol). These are not wrong by any means, but not typical in many cases either, especially for a layout that is nominally set before 1932.

Two things need to be considered: firstly, if you are working to a pre-1930 timescale, what actually happened as regards GWR passenger stock before this point? Secondly, how can this be replicated? Don't throw the above RTR models on to the fire yet; the quality of moulding is good and they can be improved. The Hornby B-set coach (more on that dubious designation later) is fairly close to a Diagram E140 bow-end coach built c.1930 and the Hornby Autocoach is a loose representation of an A28 diagram vehicle from the same period (note that the Bachmann Autocoach is a BR build from 1951). Both of these can be worked on by the modeller and are ideal for a western section based layout set post-1931, but what if your layout represents an earlier period and a different area?

There were a small number of coaches designed and built by the GWR specifically for branch-line work, but what was more common was 'cascading'. In common with all other companies, the GWR constantly upgraded and modernized its coaching stock. A large amount of this stock was scrapped upon withdrawal, but some items would be put out to grass pottering up and down a rural branch. This meant that suitable coaches (often non-corridor van thirds) were shuffled off to the countryside to end their days tacked on to cattle wagons and being used as extra braking power on mixed trains (a mixed train being a combination of coaches and non-express passenger train rated wagons).

What was more likely on a branch before the 1930s was initially four-wheel ex-fast commuter stock and later panelled bogie coaches with either clerestories or arc roofs. Does this suggest a tidy split of styles? Not in the slightest – the GWR was quite happy to grab whatever suitable stock was available and mixing the three styles in one train was com-

monplace. In other words, as a modeller you can get away with most things providing you stay roughly in period. Mixing four-wheel, six-wheel and clerestory stock looks logical; but mixing four-wheel stock with 1930s bow-ended smooth-panelled stock doesn't.

ABSORBED COACHING STOCK

The final consideration is the GWR's use of absorbed coaching stock. With the takeover of other company's lines, the GWR found itself owning extra good-quality coaching stock that was relatively new, low mileage and ideal for branch work (often on its home line), the most obvious being the ex-Barry Railway brake third that ran on the Culm Valley branch for many years. Modelling these types takes a little more research, but does take you away from the more obvious and common choices.

WHAT'S AVAILABLE TO USE FOR MODELLING?

The challenge for the modeller is to research and build suitable passenger stock for the area and period modelled. There is quite a bit of help to build the earlier stock, starting with the rather ubiquitous Ratio range of four-wheel coaches. These are based closely on a prototype diagram, but part of their beauty is that they are made from standard-size panels and therefore are ideal for chopping up into other types. The other useful item here is the Tri-ang (later Hornby) clerestory bogie coach – that is, the older moulded version, not the later versions with

Tip

Look out for old Ratio kits or Tri-ang clerestories at exhibitions. They have been around a long time and damaged examples with broken coupling and buffers can be picked up for next to nothing. As they will be chopped up for body parts, this probably won't matter.

the panels simply printed on. These can be picked up quite cheaply second-hand and make excellent modelling source material.

Note: Although the standard designation for a coach with both a passenger section and a luggage/guard section is usually 'brake third', the GWR insisted in some cases to refer to this type as 'van third'. This may have some historical root, but also may have been to indicate that there was a portion of the passenger train that contained a section where parcels, luggage and light goods could be carried.

PROJECT THREE: W1 PASSENGER VAN

In recent years, the GWR Ratio four-wheel coach kits have been augmented by a range of brass parts and overlays from Shire Scenes. These are excellent products, but include the word 'brass', which scares many people off. Most are happy to work with plastic, but the fear of using metal makes the kits appear too hard. If this describes you, there is another way by using extra plastic coach sides which are available as spares to convert the Ratio coaches into other types. The simplest of all of these is the W1 passenger van, which involves one join in each side and the shortening of the roof and underframe.

HISTORY

The van (there was but one) was constructed in the late nineteenth century and was still extant, albeit as a grounded body acting as a store, into the 1940s, though its use as a van in general traffic would probably have ended by the 1930s at the absolute outside. Designed to run within a rake of passenger coaches to carry parcels and other baggage, it was originally fitted with oil lamp roof equipment, but this was removed when gas lighting was introduced. It is unclear from the standard drawing, or from the 1947 photo available, if gas lamps were added instead (*see below* for ideas about how to approach this). Its use on branches, if at all, is undocumented, but it was common to

downgrade passenger vans for use such as transporting fruit and other produce, so there is a reasonable excuse for using one for later periods. However, it will fit perfectly within a rake of four- and six-wheel coaches in an earlier timeframe. The reason for using it here is to demonstrate a simple way to get the modeller to try some 'cut and shut' techniques to alter commercial coach kits. The techniques used will happily transfer to any scale.

Materials required:
• Ratio Models brake third coach, Ref: 613
• Extra sides for the same. Available direct from Ratio Models or from Dundas Models of Fife
• Plastic strip 10 × 20thou
• Scrap plastic
• Liquid solvent and all-purpose adhesive
• Blu-tack
• Paint.

Tools required:
• Sanding stick and files
• Knife or scalpel
• 2mm and 1mm drills
• Razor saw (X-Acto)
• Brushes.

CUTTING AND SHUTTING

Essentially what we are doing here is cutting off two pairs of luggage ends from four sides and rejoining to make one shorter van. Cut the sides as marked using a razor saw, cutting one piece on the waste side of the vertical framing and the other down the middle of the framing. The passenger seating ends can be put in the spares box.

Make sure that the cuts are dead square and join the two sections using liquid solvent. Note there is likely to be a little discrepancy top and bottom due to moulding variation. This can be smoothed later – just make sure that the raised framing on the face lines up. Add a piece of scrap plastic at the rear of the join to make it stronger and let the join harden for a while. Repeat the process with the other pair of sides.

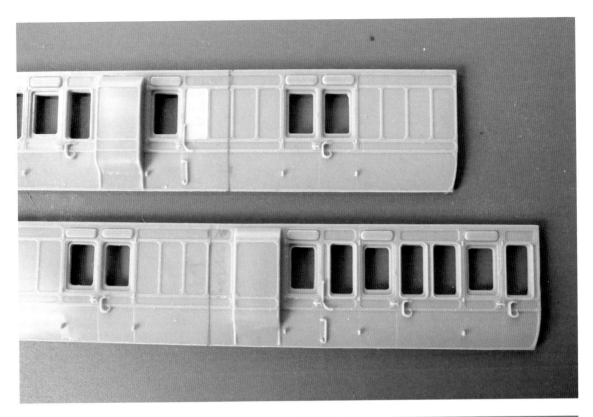

Cutting marks. The right-hand end of the lower side is waste and the left in the upper is waste.

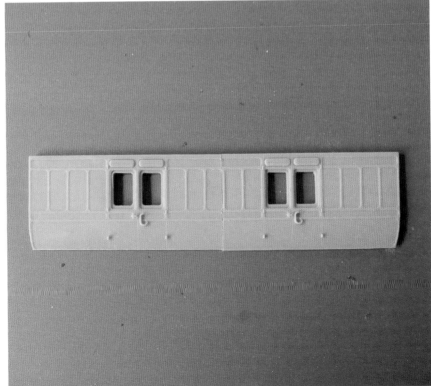

Get the framing in the centre lined up – the lower edge can be tidied up later.

Painting Suggestion

The combined sides are best painted before full assembly as they can be kept flat. First of all, paint the framing black (33) and let it dry. Then using a 'float' technique, add a slightly dilute drop of Cream (103) paint into a panel and move the paint into the corners with a small brush. The surface tension should do most of the work for you. Add more paint as required. There are several videos on the Internet which demonstrate this, so it may be worth taking a look at these first. Take your time through this process – painting panelled coaches is not for the faint-hearted, but have a go, or start with a little practice on the scrap passenger ends that you've cut off.

Follow this with Pullman Umber Brown Acrylic Paint (Humbrol RC 415) for the lower panels. When dry, add Brick Red (70) to the drop-light frames on the two doors.

Four-wheel luggage van showing early lining style.

Saloon coach showing simplified lining.

UNDERFRAME

The kit underframe is set at a scale 19ft (5,791mm) wheelbase and needs to be reduced to 16ft (4,877mm). Therefore, a 12mm section needs to be removed from the centre. Mark 6mm either side of the centre and carefully cut the solebar/step with a razor saw. Cut the tie bar with a knife, then reassemble, checking that the wheelbase is 64mm. Repeat with the second solebar, making sure that it matches the first's wheelbase exactly. A millimetre out on both won't notice, but skewed axles will, so the matching of both is more important. Add the bearings, noting that this kit shares the same problem as the Ratio open wagon built earlier, in that the bearings will need to sit slightly proud of the plastic in order to hold the standard metal axles. Refer to Chapter Three to see this.

FLOOR

Take the floor piece and clean off any flash. As the floor will be shortened, none of the moulded markings will have any relevance, so file the bottom of the floor smooth. Trim the length to about 98mm as shown and clean up. Keep checking this length against the sides, noting that the floor section drops into a rebate on the end pieces and that a new semi-circular end notch needs to be made.

Solebar assembly with section removed.

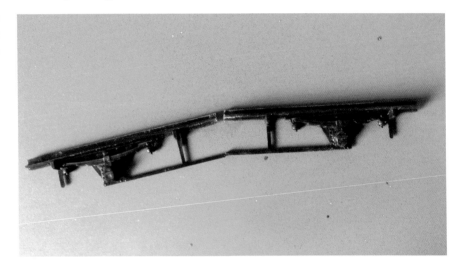

Floor with section removed and new 'notch' cut in end.

Tip

It is often worth just tacking the extreme ends of the solebars to the floor with solvent and seeing if the vehicle will run true through some point-work before fixing them firmly. It is much easier to break a tiny glue joint at this point and then to reset it, rather than bin the entire kit because it won't run properly. Also check that all wheels touch the ground using a flat surface. This gets particularly more problematic as model wheel-bases get longer.

Add one end to one side, followed by the second end, using the floor as a guide and removing any material from the floor if necessary. Check that the assembly is square at all times. Spring the shortened floor piece into place and add the second side.

Take the assembled shortened solebars, line them up centrally against the floor and mark where to trim the ends. The original is slightly offset, so this is likely to be in the region of 3mm from one end and 5mm from the other. Repeat with the other side in MIRROR form. Check that the axle boxes are still directly opposite each other. Add the reduced solebars to the floor, using the remaining redundant location hole as a guide and trap the wheel sets between. This may need a bit of juggling to get right and as with previous kits the use of Blu-tack to hold one side while the other is positioned may be helpful.

INSIDE THE VAN

The W1 vans were fitted with a system of shelves around the edges which could be added should you wish, though it's unlikely that they will be able to be seen, so in this case they can probably be omitted.

Add some weight to the floor of the van. Here, a small strip of roofing lead has been used. An alternative would be the lead strip sold by pet shops

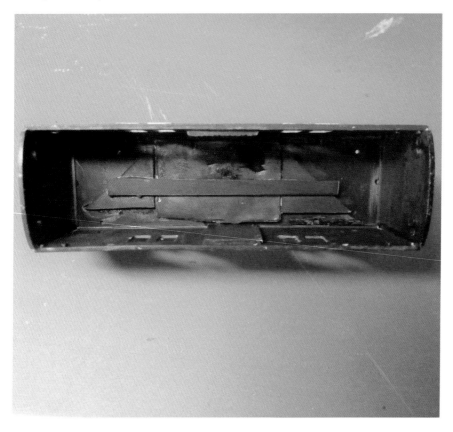

Internal view showing weight trapped with scrap plastic sheet.

The inside of the roof should be given a rough coat of black. Note the right-hand end is slightly feathered.

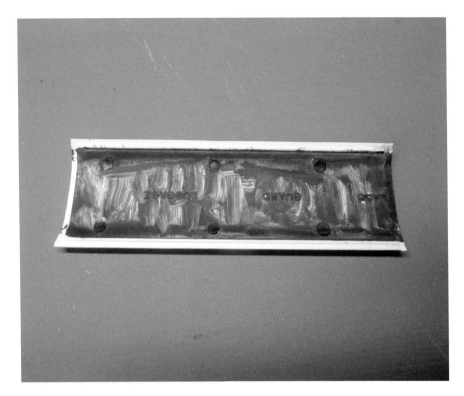

for weighting aquarium features. The lead should be stuck down, but it's a pretty safe bet that this will come loose once the roof is fixed, so here it is trapped between scrap plastic to make sure it stays put. Then give the whole of the interior a sloppy coat of black paint. This is to make the van interior appear dark by removing any light refection.

Glazing can now be added from the strips included in the kit. About a 25–30mm length should be adequate. Use all-purpose adhesive, but make sure that the glue does not spread over the window aperture.

ROOF AND LIGHTING

Working on any historical model has pitfalls and questions involved, and this is no exception. While the post-1920s rolling stock is quite well documented, the late nineteenth-century items are less so, thus a degree of supposition is required. While the panelling and shelving are described, what happened on the roof and under the floor is a little hazy. The vans were originally fitted with three 'pots' for oil lamps – one mounted dead centre, with the other two over the panels outside the outer doors. Shortly after

the van was built, the GWR started fitting coaching stock with gas lighting and much of the similar four-wheel stock (and indeed the donor kit) were so fitted. However, there is no working photograph showing this van with gas lighting. This doesn't mean that it wasn't; just that the historical evidence is sketchy. Therefore, the modeller has three options at this point: 1. Fit pots for oil lamps, which would give a period feel; 2. Assume that gas was added and fit gas lamps in similar positions; 3. Assume that the oil lamps were removed, but allowing for the fact that this passenger van was fairly low in the pecking order, that gas was not subsequently fitted. For simplicity and economy, the third option was taken here. (Parts for the first two options are available from Dart Castings and other parts suppliers.)

In common with the rest of the parts, the roof needs to be reduced in length here to 103mm, giving an overhang of 1mm at each end. The lamps on the roof would now be in the wrong place, so the first procedure is to sand the roof flat. You will have lost the rebate that drops over the end by shortening, so 'feather' the new end with a round needle file to

Tip

One thing that study of Victorian and Edwardian period GWR photos shows, is the common misconception of roof colour. Many of these photos are 'local station postcard' shots taken from bridges. This shows the roof colour perfectly. The rose-tinted railway enthusiast's idea that coach roofs are pure white is quickly dispelled, as they mostly appear as a dirty grey tone. They may have been white when first built, but the in-service photos tell a different tale.

reduce the thickness and reduce the length of the two edge location strips. Then give the underside a sloppy coat of black, as with the rest of the inside.

Give the roof top a light coat of Tank Grey (67), let it dry thoroughly and then give it a light sanding to level. Then add two lengths of 10 × 20thou plastic strip at the ends to represent the canvas retainer. Add a second coat of paint, followed by a wash of Dark Earth (29) and add the finished roof to the coach. Hopefully the roof should fit well, so a dab of all-purpose adhesive in the corners should suffice.

UNDERSIDE FITTINGS

The footboards can now be added. Cut one end next to the second hanger and locate it over the

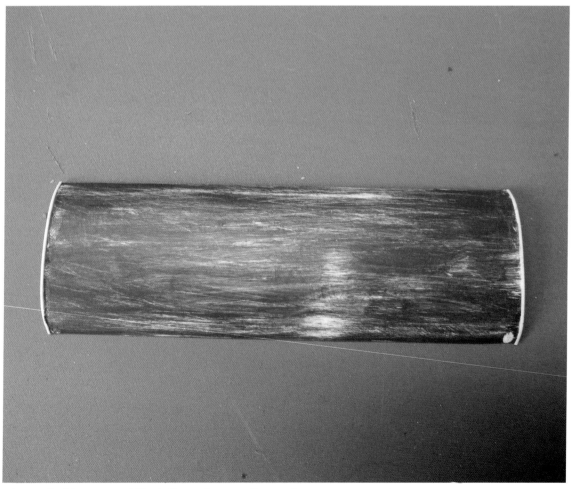

The roof with a coat of Tank Grey after sanding and new canvas retainers added from plastic strip.

Underside with one solebar fitted.

Right-hand section of footstep is fixed; the left-hand section is sized up to mark the correct length.

Brakes should be added, making sure that there is a little clearance.

Buffers and vacuum pipe added.

Completed WI luggage van.

axle box. Then trim the end to suit and gently round the corner using a sanding stick. Then take the other end and locate it in position over the axle box. Mark where the overlap occurs and trim off the excess. Give yourself a little wiggle room by not cutting too close, then sand back gradually so that the fit is good. Trim the outside end as before. Then add this second part. Repeat with the other side.

The brake shoe parts can now be attached, making sure that the wheels still spin freely. Then add the V-hanger in a central position on one side, followed by the cylinder, which should sit level with the end of the arm and 5mm inboard.

Finally, the buffers and vacuum pipes can be added. The buffers will need some gentle cleaning up and you may wish to replace these with some superior white-metal or brass examples. The painting of the underframe will be similar to the open and brake van treated earlier.

Tip

Although this conversion stands alone, it will sit well with the rest of the range of Ratio four-wheel coaches. It may be beneficial to build at least one of these coaches as per the instructions beforehand to familiarize yourself with the building order, using the above suggestions to assist.

Many further variations of the four- and six-wheel GWR coaches can be built in a similar fashion and much information and inspiration can be found in J.H. Russell's two-volume book on the subject, A Pictorial Record of Great Western Coaches.

PROJECT FOUR: HORNBY/ AIRFIX B-SET COACH

The Hornby (originally Airfix) B-set coach has been available since the early 1980s. The designation and prototype root of the model are somewhat contentious. The term 'set' on the prototype railway meant just that – a fixed set of coaches. The confusion is added when you find that the operating sections of the GWR, for example London, Birmingham and so on, had different ways of applying the term; for instance, the Birmingham section referred to the two-coach suburban set as 'D', not 'B'. For the purposes of this book and simplicity's sake, the term 'B' can be taken to refer to a pair of van composites run in fixed formation.

The confusion for the novice is that it is assumed that the 'B' is a specific coach, which it is not; theoretically, the B is any matched pair of van composites, and not a particular coach. That being the first level of confusion, the second is that the AIrfix/ Hornby model is an amalgam of two or three different designs (diagrams). If you start scratching the surface, you will find that there are heated opinions on Internet forums as to which diagram it actually represents. There are three possibilities, which are

Examples of GWR coach set consists from the London Division (other divisions varied):

- 4 Coach A-Set Electric Lighting: Van 3rd (6 compartments), First (8 compts), Third (9 compts), Van 3rd (6 compts)
- 5 coach A-Set Ordinary Stock: Van 3rd, Third, First, Third, Van 3rd
- B-Set Electric Lighting: Van Compo, Van Compo (Van Compos to have one 1st and 5 × 3rd compartments in each coach)
- C-Set Ordinary Stock: Van 3rd, Third, First, Lav Compo, Van 3rd
- D-Set Ordinary Stock: Van 3rd, Compo, Compo, Van 3rd
- E-Set Ordinary Stock: Van 3rd, First, Third, Van 3rd
- G-Set Ordinary Stock: Van 3rd, Third, Compo (3), Van.
- H-Set Ordinary Stock: Van 3rd, Lav Compo, Van 3rd.

B-set coach as supplied.

diag. E140, E147 or E145. Much of the Airfix coach resembles an E140, though there are errors – length, recessed door handles, truss rods and so on. A lot of this comes down to the 1980s production techniques, which were very good at the time, and the fact that it shared some parts with the same company's Centenary coach model. Lastly, photographs of working branch trains point to the use of mostly flat-ended stock, whereas the Airfix model is of the bow-ended type.

The modeller therefore has choices: ignore all the discrepancies and run the model as it is; change a few things to make it more like the E140 diagram; or start from scratch and buy a kit of the correct coach. Here it was decided to take the basic easily available model and upgrade it slightly to lift it away from all the other Airfix B-sets, but without plumping for the more drastic surgery of a conversion or fully etched brass kit that would discourage the novice modeller. The big advantage is that not only is it available new from Hornby, but the original Airfix models can be picked up unboxed, but in good condition, at exhibitions or on Internet auction sites for as little as £5.00, making it a good way to dip your toe in the water and try out a couple of new techniques without a large cash outlay.

Materials required:
- Airfix/Hornby B-set suburban coach
- MJT buffers ref 2330S (Dart Castings)
- 40thou plastic sheet
- Scrap plastic
- Brake and heating pipes (optional) (Dart Castings)
- Solvent and all-purpose adhesive
- Paint.

Tools required:
- Craft knife
- Needle files/sanding stick
- Razor saw
- Drills – 2mm and 0.8mm
- Brushes.

OPENING UP THE COACH

The first thing to do is to get the coach apart. The bogies and coupling simply pull off. The body is held on by three step clips per side, which join the seating to the glazing. The best way to release this is to insert a knife blade under the body side, twist slightly and ease the body off. This is fraught with danger, as it is possible to slip and damage the paintwork, or worse, slip and remove a fingertip. PLEASE TAKE CARE. The seating is fixed to the underframe by five screws.

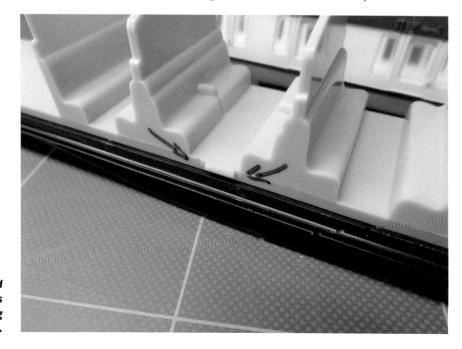

The body is held by three step clips on the seating moulding.

CHANGING THE HEADSTOCK

If we assume that the coach is a bow-ended E140, then the headstock (buffer beam) is wrong, as it needs to be flat and not curved in line with the end of the body. This is easily replaced with plastic.

Make two diagonal saw cuts at each side of the headstock with a razor saw, but only to the depth of the headstock, not to the floor. Then remove the headstock with the saw, using the mould line as a guide.

Final cut to remove headstock.

End smoothed, showing curve of end.

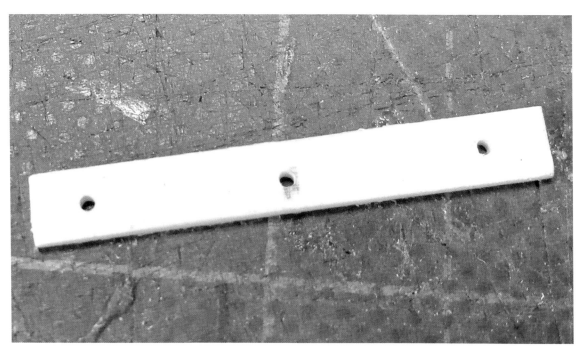

New headstock with pilot holes drilled.

Headstock fitted and reinforced with scrap plastic.

LEFT: *Door droplights can be touched in with Brick Red for a late-period coach.*

OPPOSITE: *Completed B-set coach.*

Cut a new piece from 40thou sheet to match your gap, which should be around 30mm long by 4mm deep. Trial-fit this piece and mark the centre using the bogie pivot hole as a guide. Then make two marks either side 12.5mm from this centre mark. Find the vertical centre line and drill pilot holes in all three. Trial-fit again to see if this looks right. If all is well, open up the outer holes using a 2mm drill. Smear a thin coat of all-purpose adhesive around the new gap in the floor, let it go off, then add the new part using solvent. Make sure that it is upright and add some reinforcing pieces from scrap plastic or sprue.

The MJT buffer stocks can now be fitted after they have had their holes drilled through to clear and been have cleaned up. The buffer heads are best left until last, as they are easily damaged during the rest of the work. When fully set, these new parts should be given a thin coat of Tank Grey paint.

BODY

The Airfix coach body is printed using the technique of the day. This is neatly done, but when the glazing is removed (by pushing gently inward), it is notice-

able that the window reveals are not coloured and neither are the droplight windows on the doors. It is doubtful whether most modellers would be able to match even this 1980s finish with the long straight line between two colours and the dozen or so sets of lettering per side. In this case, it was decided to leave the main colouring and just add some paint detailing. With the coach sides, just touching in the door drop-lights with Brick Red (70) using a small brush changes the look of the body straight away.

ROOF

As with the W1 luggage van described earlier, the roof should be first given a couple of thin coats of Tank Grey (67) to cover the white plastic, and after this has dried thoroughly given a wash of Dark Earth (29). The only physical modification is to sand off the moulding pip in the centre.

INTERIOR AND FINISHING

The seating colours changed from a deep red in the early years of GWR coaches through to a brown. This coach would likely be fitted with a grey cloth,

so the ends of the seats, the floors and bulkheads should be painted a red-brown colour and the seats themselves given a coat of mid-grey.

The underframe and bogies can also be treated with the same grey/brown paintwork as the roof and when all the new paintwork has hardened the coach can be reassembled. At this juncture, the ends can also be painted dark grey and washed with brown, and finally the buffer heads can be fitted. The head-stocks carried both brake and heating pipes, and if you are using a scale coupling they should be added. Here the original tension-lock couplings have been retained, and as these would foul any added pipe-work, it has been omitted in this case.

CLOSE-COUPLING OPTION

The Hornby/Airfix B-set coach is a basically sound model, which is a boon for the novice modeller, especially for one working on a budget. A pair could easily run the service on a late-period model branch until more accurate coaches can be constructed. There is also an option of single coach running – most sets were close-coupled with a shorter set of buffers between (these are also available from MJT), but some were built with standard couplings as used in this project, allowing them to be run either independently or as additions to bolster other sets.

CHAPTER FIVE

APPROACHING ABSORBED ROLLING STOCK

Although the GWR already had a fairly sizable fleet of rolling stock, the 1923 Grouping and various earlier acquisitions swelled these numbers by thousands. Some of this stock was quickly deemed redundant or unfit for purpose and was destroyed, but quite a large proportion of it worked to the end of its natural working life, often not straying far from its original home turf. In time, most of this stock was repainted into standard GWR colour schemes, though it would be fair to say that it wasn't regarded as generally desirable by the company and was in the main worked out of use in short order. Much of it was gradually moved into permanent way and departmental use – probably the most brutal and harsh life for any item of stock.

Typical owner wagon at Didcot Railway Centre – 9ft wheelbase, wooden solebars and at the bottom left the colliery that it should be returned to for reloading.

As far as the modeller is concerned, this intro-duces a couple of points that are worth bearing in mind. As stated earlier, the GWR took in more goods traffic from other companies than it sent out, so was caught on the wrong side of the divide with repairs under the pooling agreement. And post-Grouping, the company had these extra foreign items on its own stock list. This means that the expected stand-ard type of stock that appears on many layouts is possibly more numerous than it should be and even though it may be painted in GWR colours, the origin of the home stock is likely to be somewhere else, at least up to 1930. The question arises then of how to represent this without turning your GWR branch-line layout into something else.

Of course, this would not have been a system-wide situation. The West Country lines and those directly north of the Paddington–Bristol main line would be less affected, but on the north-west of the GWR system, where the majority of these acquisi-tions were rooted, the likelihood increases. It should be noted that the modeller should generally con-sider adding some foreign stock into the mix. The further consideration is that of coal traffic. The GWR owned but a tiny number of home-built coal wagons, the majority being (private) owner wagons, either belonging to merchants or collieries, and these were also, technically, foreign vehicles.

The above is the basic historical premise, but what is the best way to start looking at increasing the model fleet of foreign-origin rolling stock? Many of the pre-Grouping (and early GWR wagons) are avail-able from suppliers such as David Geen and 51L in 4mm scale, but most of these are of white-metal and/ or brass construction and the novice may not initially be comfortable with this form of construction. 7mm scale is awash with numerous small cottage industry suppliers who cover the same sort of types. The situ-ation is the same in N gauge, though at a substantially lower number. Joining the appropriate modelling society for your chosen scale opens up the avail ability of such items, as they are often only available, or publicized, to these closed groups. As always, the 4mm scale modeller does have a slightly easier ride and if you are prepared to do a small amount of mod-elling work yourself and accept a few compromises along the way, you will find suitable items available in your local model shop. It's just a case of having a little imagination coupled with some prototype research. The Welsh lines are particularly well covered with regard to printed material, with books available con-taining photographs and drawings of many suitable items, along with details of their later lives under the GWR umbrella.

The following two projects will cover simple kit builds and conversions in 4mm scale, which will give the modeller an easy route into adding some foreign wagons on to a GWR branch-line layout.

VARIATIONS ON A THEME

The first project in this section is a simple variation on a vehicle that was discussed earlier, the MINK. The all-metal version was built in great numbers by the GWR for its own purposes and for other rail-ways, but it was also built by other people for other railways. The vehicle dealt with here is a MINK built by Harrison and Camm in 1908 as a batch of 300 for merchants Spillers and Baker. All of these went to the GWR in 1911, except thirty that went to the Rhymney Railway, which was then subsequently absorbed by the GWR and the wagons taken into the GWR's stock. These Harrison and Camm vans were a touch lower in the body than the usual GWR design, but otherwise dimensionally similar. Axle boxes were changed during the GWR ownership and very much later the brakes were altered to meet Board of Trade regulations by having standard Morton brakes fitted on one side; though oddly only operating one shoe. Photographic evidence seems to support this, but, as with all wagon brakes, general repairs and upgrades are always subject to some question.

Although the vans are listed as lasting into the 1940s, it is doubtful whether this actually means in general service. A more likely route was that they were pushed into a secondary role of departmental stock. At least one had a hatch cut in the roof and was used as a van for carrying sawdust, although from where to where is not explained; possibly from the GWR's carriage and wagon shops to a place of disposal, although pre-war sawdust would still have had a further extensive use in the meat trade as floor covering.

PROJECT FIVE: RHYMNEY RAILWAY MINK

The Rhymney vans were at first glance identical to the standard GWR vehicle, though closer inspection gives a couple of detail differences. Some modellers may not think that these vans are worth bothering with, but they do provide a nice little modelling project and it would be possible to backdate things further by finishing the van in the Rhymney Railway livery of light grey, with RR in the place of the normal GW.

The two detail differences are both on the body and are: smaller ventilator covers on the ends; and an angled commode handle at the corner of each end. The latter are unusual in a fairly lowly goods vehicle and there is no obvious explanation as to why they should have been so fitted. The kit base for this van is the same Ratio MINK as used for the small cattle van detailed later and is freely available from all Peco stockists.

Materials required:
- Ratio Iron MINK kit, Ref: 563
- Small amount of 30thou plastic sheet
- 0.5mm handrail wire or similar
- Solvent and all-purpose adhesive or superglue
- Paint.

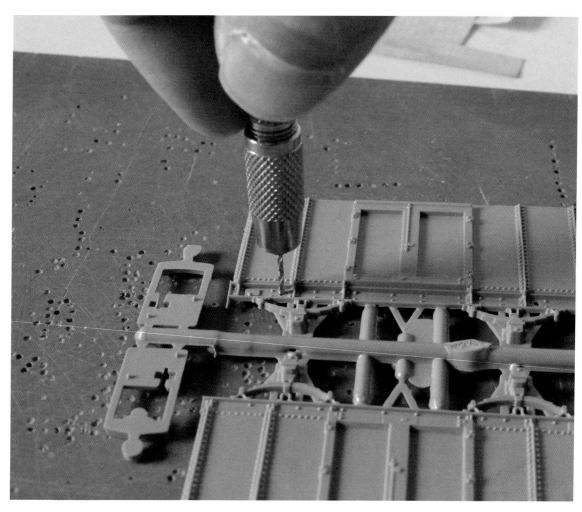

Horse hook holes can be drilled in the solebar.

Tools required:
- Pin chuck and drills
- Sanding stick
- Needle files
- Side cutters
- Brushes.

HORSE HOOKS

The first thing to tackle is the horse hooks – actually two holes on each side of the solebars. A simple 1mm drill is adequate for the job, drilling in the centre of the solebar just before the second upright from each end. Whilst working on the chassis, the axle boxes can be drilled out to 2mm and the bearings fitted as per the previous wagons.

NEW END VENTS

The end ventilator covers on the Rhymney vans were quite a bit smaller than those on the standard GWR iron MINK. The kit end has these, quite unhelpfully, moulded on, so they need to be carefully taken off. Using a flat needle file, work slowly until the vent cover is completely removed, leaving a paper-thin section. Take extra care not to damage the rivet detail on the uprights.

Cut a strip of 30thou plastic sheet 18mm long and 4mm wide. Then cut this in half to give two 9mm lengths. Holding one of these at about 25 degrees from horizontal, rub back and forth along a sanding stick until a shallow wedge shape is created (probably along with removing a layer of skin from your finger!). Repeat with the second piece and then add to the ends 2.5mm down from the top.

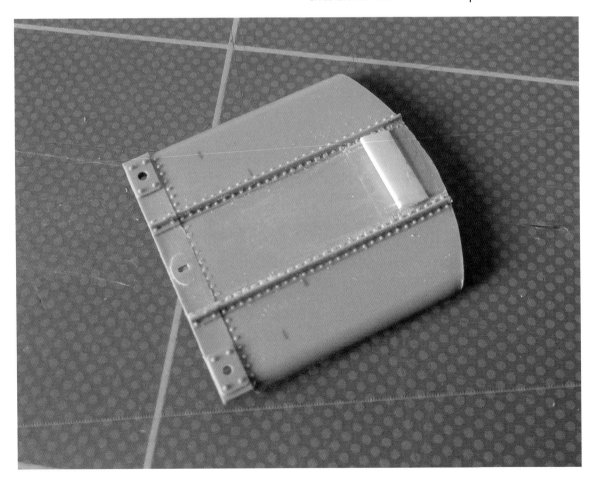

The new shorter ventilator cover added.

COMMODE HANDLES

Working from the top of the buffer beam, mark two lines – one 5mm up and one 9mm up. Using these lines as a guide, mark the positon of the ends of the handles – the lower at 2mm from the edge and the upper 6mm from the edge. Double-check all your measurements and add a pencil mark between these two points to ensure that it works visually, then drill all four mark points with a 0.5mm drill. Bend up a length of handrail wire and attach into the holes with superglue or all-purpose adhesive.

Tip

The best way to fit any of this type of handle is to create an uneven 'U' shape, consisting of one leg just over the length you need and the other with a much longer length. First, make the short bend and insert into one hole. Then mark where the second bend should be. Make this bend, but don't trim the length. Feed this 'long leg' through first, followed by the short leg and add the glue.

Leaving the long leg gives you a purchase point with which to wiggle the handle into the correct position as the glue goes off. Cutting both legs to the exact length first will leave you less control over the precise position. When the glue has hardened, trim the excess from the long leg with a pair of side cutters.

The rest of the assembly can be carried out as per the printed instructions, though there are two further suggestions. Firstly, the ends, sides and floor are quite a tight fit, especially on length. It is worth reducing the length of the floor by about 1mm at each end. This means that this part is no longer an interfering factor. Secondly, the sides have a lip that overlaps the ends. In order to make this join snug, give the face of the ends a couple of sanding-stick strokes at the point where the lip attaches.

PAINTING

When complete, the van can be painted all over in GWR standard freight grey (Humbrol 67). The roofs were originally white, but as with previous vehicles this can be darkened to a mid-grey (Humbrol 27). The position of the lettering was in standard positions and the GWR numbered the ex-Rhymney vans in the range 100924–53. A number can be made up reasonably easily from the sheet supplied by cutting out individual numbers from the given sets, though it is a bit of a squeeze space-wise. The van can be given a light coat of varnish (Humbrol 49), then lightly weathered.

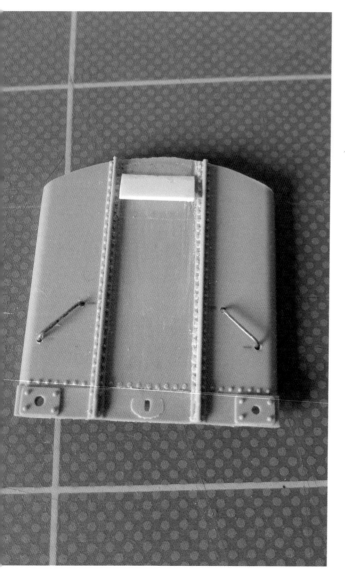

Commode handles are added on each end.

The completed ex-Spillars/Rhymney Railway van.

AN ABSORBED DEPARTMENTAL WAGON

Pre-group wagons are very thin on the ground in plastic kit form, mainly being the preserve of metal kits. These are not always easy to obtain and many novice modellers shy away from them preferring to stay in the comfort of plastic. One company that does produce a few suitable kits is Cambrian Models. These are available in many model shops and also through their website. Two of these kits are of Cambrian Railways prototypes and one can be built, or indeed converted to fit our subject.

HISTORY

Between 1896 and 1904, the Cambrian Railways built a large number of two-plank drop-side wagons for transporting high-mass, low-bulk loads. These were largely used for transporting slate, which creates a dense, heavy load that does not require a high-sided vehicle. These worked mainly from the trans-shipment stations in Mid and North Wales. At the 1923 Grouping, these wagons were taken into GWR stock

and were quickly transferred in the main to departmental use. Little work was done to the wagons, except adding corner plates to some, which fixed the drop-side doors in place. This may seem odd, but it may have been a way of prolonging the life of the wagons, as the doors on a drop side are prone to early failure due to hard usage. The other reason may be that the GWR saw the benefit of a low fixed-side wagon; shovelling ballast out of a drop side makes sense, but having a number of vehicles that were able to be loaded with time-expired sleepers and rail fixings from the trackside by the permanent way gangs, would have been seen as a cheap and almost throwaway option.

PROJECT SIX: ALTERED CAMBRIAN RAILWAYS DROP-SIDE WAGON

Materials required:
- Cambrian Models Cambrian Railways two-plank drop-side wagon, Ref: C100
- Small amount of 10thou plastic sheet

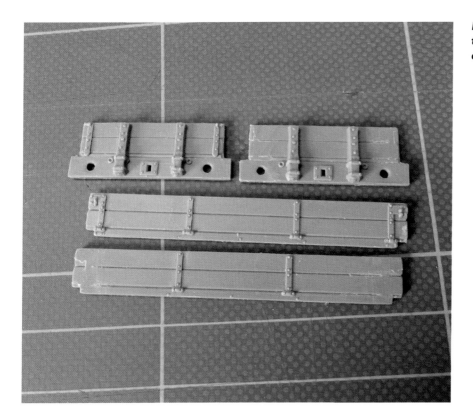

Body parts showing the original details and after removal.

- Spoked wheels and bearings
- Transfers
- Turned buffer heads (optional)
- Solvent and gel superglue
- Paint.

Tools required:
- Knife
- Sanding stick and needle files
- Drills
- Household needle
- Brushes.

WORKING TOWARD THE GWR UPGRADE

The Cambrian Models kits are made from a softer plastic than other similar kits, therefore the moulding is generally not as sharp, although with care they produce as good a finished item as the more cleanly moulded kits from Ratio, Parkside and the like. They are also a little cheaper, but do not include wheels or transfers, which have to be sourced separately.

This can be an advantage, as you are able to make substitutions to these with less waste. Having a less complete kit gives you more freedom.

The Great Western's upgrade of adding corner plates is an easy alteration. The primary task is to remove the long hinge plates from each end of the side pieces, as well as the bracing plates from the end pieces. This can be done by making gentle flat strokes with a needle file until the moulding is flush with the planking. Take care not to drift away from the actual moulding toward the centre, as you do not want to damage or smooth the plank lines. The side and end parts can be cleaned up as normal and put to one side.

CHASSIS

As with previous kits, the chassis parts can now be built up and checked for even and smooth running before any body parts are added. The recommended Gibson wheel sets were used here and there was no need to make any adjustment to the placing of the solebars or the position of the brass bearings.

The chassis constructed and the ends added.

CONSTRUCTION

Trial-fit all the body parts. The floor is about 1mm too long for a snug fit of the step in the side pieces, so after checking this carefully remove 0.5mm from each end. Then add the end pieces, making sure that they line up exactly with the edge line of the floor.

Finally, trial-fit the sides again, removing any material that extends past the already fitted ends; the corner must be square. When you are satisfied that all is well, fix the sides to the ends, but do not add solvent along the floor line – there should be a tiny gap.

CORNER PLATES

Cut a section of 10thou plastic sheet 6.5mm wide by 34mm long. On one side mark three lines at 8.5mm intervals. Also mark a centre line to act as a visual guide. Then using an ordinary household needle in a pin chuck make four 'dents' evenly in each quadrant. It does not matter if you push right through as the paint will fill the hole, but fairly light pressure will create the right effect. When you have

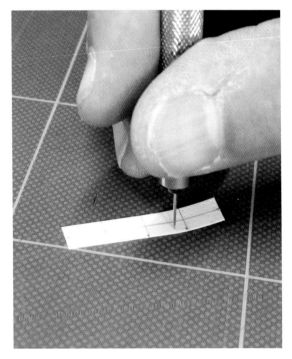

Using a needle held in a pin chuck to create 'rivets' in the corner plates.

The body now constructed with new corner plates.

worked your way right along, mark halfway along each 8.5mm section and lightly scribe a line. This will form the fold of each corner plate. Finally, cut the four pieces from the strip and very gently bend each one into a right angle. Add one plate to each corner of the wagon.

FINISHING OFF

The single-sided Morton brake gear can now be added. The buffers had their base plates extended by the Cambrian and these should be added. The easiest way to do this is to leave the small square extension plates on the sprue and fix the buffer stocks to these in situ. This is better than trying to hold both parts

Tip

When adding any sort of plastic patch to a plastic kit as in this instance, use only a fine non-plastic item such as the tip of a knife blade to hold the part in place. Don't whatever you do use your finger tip. The likelihood is that the capillary action of the solvent will find it and you will end up with a beautifully moulded fingerprint on the surface of your model, rendering it totally useless.

together when loose. The completed part can be cut from the sprue and cleaned up when set.

It was decided here to replace the plastic buffer heads with some turned steel ones from Keen-Maygib, which give a much finer overall finish. This meant that the buffer stocks needed to be drilled through at 0.7mm. The tiny collars were left on the sprue, drilled 0.7mm and the new buffer heads were threaded through and fixed with gel superglue. When set, they were added to the buffer stocks and the entire assemblies fitted to the wagon. This is very much an optional operation, but does give a finer finished article for quite low extra expense.

The wagon can now be painted and finished in the usual manner. Transfers can be sourced from Fox or Model Master, or made up as here from spare Ratio characters.

If you wished to run a usefully short engineer's train on your layout, it could consist of a pair of these wagons (one built as per the instructions and one as detailed here), accompanied by one of the pure GWR ballast wagons (also available from Cambrian Models) and an older style – possibly a wooden out-side-framed GWR brake van.

If you are working in N gauge, this two-plank drop-side vehicle would make an easy first try in scratch-building, using a Peco 9ft wheelbase chassis kit as a foundation.

The completed ex-Cambrian Railways open.

OTHER PRE-GROUPING WAGON IDEAS

If you have a desire to turn the clock back slightly from most GWR layouts, which tend to be set in the 1930s, the starting point need not be too far from your nearest model shop. The Cambrian Railways drop side detailed above is an easily obtainable kit, but there are others lurking in the 4mm OO plastic ranges. Ratio produces a set of London & North Western Railway open wagons in a single set, which may be quite useful should you set your layout in the Midlands area. The Southern Railway box van is a South Eastern & Chatham design and could be back-dated, while there are several pre-Grouping designs of other Southern area wagons from the London, Brighton & South Coast Railway and the London & South Western Railway from Cambrian Models, which may be suitable if you were setting your line in the south-west.

As an aside, the Ratio Models Southern van is an iconic design for that railway, but in 1942 a batch of 650 was built for the GWR at Ashford in Kent and designated a diagram number of V35. If you were keen to start a heated discussion and possibly win a wager or two, then one of these lettered in the GWR's final small letter style and placed on a late-period layout could be quite fun.

This chapter barely scratches the surface of the thousands of goods and passenger vehicles that the GWR inherited, absorbed and acquired. Researching these would be a life's study and modelling them would be another, but including just a few on your layout will make it a little different from the usual models of the GWR.

CHAPTER SIX

BRANCH-LINE LOCOMOTIVES

FIRST CONSIDERATIONS

Everyone knows which locomotives worked on GWR branches, don't they? The opening chapter blows a couple of these preconceptions away, but most of them are fairly accurate, especially for the post-1930 period. In the main, there are some basic rules: small tank locomotives – usually four or six coupled wheel types, often running a specific branch route all day. There are also some general geographical rules: to the north and south of the London– Bristol main line (or the M4 motorway if you prefer), there were certain types that predominated. To the south (Thames Valley, Devon, Cornwall and so on), the branches of the GWR were mostly worked by 0-4-2 side tanks and 2-6-2 prairie tanks, with the 48XX and 44XX or 45XX being common in later years. North of this invisible line, pannier tanks held sway. That is not to say that these particular classes could not be seen in the other area, just that this was more typical.

There were also other general area-typical classes: the Forrest of Dean was almost exclusively worked by pannier tanks, while the short, steep branches of South Wales were mostly worked by 0-6-2 heavy tank engines. West Wales, on the other hand, saw more in the way of light tender engine use, due in part to the preference of the Cambrian Railways for these.

What this means for the modeller is yet more detailed research if a certain area is to be accurately portrayed. No one is going to report you to the authorities for running the wrong locomotives, but if you announce that your branch-line model is set in deepest Cornwall, then produce a 56XX 0-6-2 tank locomotive, it will jar just as much as if you had produced the *Flying Scotsman*. The 56XX is by no means totally impossible in that scenario, but it is

less likely. Likewise, 48XX 0-4-2 tanks did run some light passenger services in South Wales, but always looked slightly embarrassed about it, being surrounded by much beefier power. It is, then, mostly about getting the typicality right – the right engine in the right place. Not only will this please the more knowledgeable viewer, but it will more than likely be more satisfying for the modeller. If you have taken the trouble to get the buildings and the track plan correct, you may as well go the whole hog and get the motive power correct too. It's all about creating a complete picture on your layout.

BACKDATING

The above information is very much swayed toward the later periods, but what about pre-1930? To some extent the same general rules hold true, but the locomotive classes change. The prairie tanks were quite an old design (the turn of the twentieth century) so they will still fit, as will some panniers; though the further back you go, the more likely they are to be saddle tank versions and/or outside-framed (the chassis frames set outside of the wheels). The 0-4-2 48XX can be directly swapped for a 517 class or a Metro tank.

For both the early and later periods (1930 is a comfortable dividing line), studying the shed allocations for the area that you are modelling is a good place to start, as it would be doubtful that a branch engine would have been drawn from much further afield than its local motive power depot (MPD). There are wild cards that can be played if you fancy a change – line testing is one, engineering trains from a different area is another, but if you are modelling a rural single-track branch line, due to weight and speed restrictions, the range of motive power classes would have been fairly small, especially as the country branches may only have clung on to one or two engines for many years.

BUDGET MODELLING

This last point is actually the root of the whole branch modelling genre. What the low selection of motive power gives you is the time to work up a small stud of locos, with real coal added and all the proper pipework, crew and so on. Two locomotives, a rake or two of coaches, plus a dozen or so wagons would be enough to keep most modellers busy for a year or more. Highly enjoyable and a fairly low strain on the household budget. Buying the latest RTR model is good retail therapy, but in this instance looking around for those slightly older, but still very good quality models (such as the B-set coach treated earlier), is sound practice, as these will be able to take more 'modelling' and will usually be a cheaper long-term option.

The next project is just that sort of option – low on initial cost, but high on modelling time spent working it up into something more realistic and personal to you. Of course, if you are fortunate enough to have a good supply of spare cash and are short of time, then the reverse applies. You can pay someone else to do the work for you and fill your layout quickly with high-quality bought-in items.

PROJECT SEVEN: AIRFIX/ HORNBY CLASS 48XX

PROTOTYPE HISTORY

With regard to small GWR engines, the 48XX comes second only to the panniers in familiarity terms, although there is once again a fair amount of misconception here, again perpetuated by numerous and long-standing model company labelling. The 48XX 0-4-2 tanks were built between 1932 and 1936, and were designed almost definitively to replace the worn-out 517 class that had been the mainstay of light passenger work. The 48XX was

1450 (originally 4850) showing a lack of top feed, fireman's bunker steps, forward-mounted toolbox and auto-control gear between the coupling and buffer stock.

Rear of 1450, showing fire iron hooks.

therefore not really a totally new design, but retained significant elements of the 517, along with a standard Collet-shape cab. The class was highly successful in its expected local passenger and shunting duties and was retained for the same type of work by British Railways right up until the mid-1960s.

The confusion comes with the classes' numbering. From 1932–46, the 48XX number range was used. This changed following World War II in 1946, when this number range was moved to the short-lived 2-8-0 oil-burning locomotives. At this point, the original numbers from some of the 517 tank class were adopted, with the result that the whole class of seventy-five engines changed from 48XX to 14XX. This means that unless you are modelling the GWR in a slim date window between 1946 and 1948 and your locomotive is numbered 14XX … it's wrong. The reason for this misconception is two-fold: the class actually carried the 14XX range for more years post-war than 48XX in total, so they have become more commonly referred to by that prefix. Secondly, the model manufacturers have traditionally saved production costs by only using the 14XX plates and labelling thus, as this will cover both GWR and BR periods … but only just. In a nutshell, if, as most do, you are modelling the GWR pre-1946, your loco needs to carry the 48 prefix and not 14.

There is one final numbering consideration. The 48XXs were fitted with mechanical linkage for use with push-pull auto-trailer coaching stock, but there were two further small batches of near identical locomotives built in 1933 that were destined for more lowly shunting work and were not fitted with this facility. These two batches of engines were numbered 5800–5819, were not changed to the 14XX range and remained 58XX for the rest of their working lives. However, there is anecdotal information that the auto-fitted/non-auto-fitted break was sometimes not as clear-cut as first seen. As usual, research into any particular locomotive would be needed to establish what was supplied, when and for how long.

MODEL OPTIONS FOR THE 48XX

Starting at the smaller scale end, a 48XX is produced by Dapol for N gauge in both British Railways and GWR liveries. Going much larger, there is a kit from Springside in O gauge (and possibly an RTR model from Dapol). In 4mm scale, there is also an aesthetically superb 48XX from DJ Models and the 48XX has long been produced, firstly by Airfix in the 1980s and this model has now been re-marketed and re-chassied by Hornby with a neater motor and pick-ups. The original Airfix drive system was through gears and a universal joint, which could in time cause

Comparison between the original Airfix (lower) and current Hornby 48XX chassis.

problems. The Hornby version uses a more standard gear arrangement. There have also been several kits marketed in 4mm scale over the years, notably from Wills/South East Finecast.

WORKING ON THE HORNBY RTR MODEL

The body moulding for both the Airfix/Hornby RTR models is identical and this is where most of the improvement work can be done. Much of this involves the removal of plastic, so you may wish to search for a second-hand example, or buy a separate body moulding to work on if you are a little nervous about chopping into a new model.

THE DIFFERENCES

The Airfix/Hornby mould is dimensionally accurate, but can be altered to suit specific locomotives. The fairly large class held several build differences and these were further added to by the 1940s. The main points to note are: top-feed; whistle shield; bunker steps; and toolboxes. Items possibly lacking in the model are: bunker tool clips; and one auto-gear cover. The top feed was initially added to some of the class and is present on the model, but the whistle shield was a much later addition, as were the bunker steps. The toolboxes were either set slightly forward

on the front splashers, or centrally to these as on the model. There is also a run of electrical cable down the offside of the cab, which is a later addition. The well-worn advice is to find a photo of your chosen loco and copy it; this advice still holds up very well. The decision here was to convert the model to 4800, the first of the class, using a second-hand Airfix body mould, which could then simply be retro-fitted to the superior Hornby chassis. Therefore, all the later additions needed to be removed, excepting the toolbox, which is correct for this particular locomotive.

Attacking a perfectly functional model locomotive with knife and files is not everyone's cup of tea and many are nervous about doing so in case they ruin the model. The advantage with this particular model is that it is available fairly cheaply, so there will hopefully be a little less fear about altering it – less than doing the same to a brand-new model costing over £100. The advice is to take your time, work through each section carefully and congratulate yourself when it all goes as planned.

Materials required:
• Airfix or Hornby 14XX body
• Chassis for same, but this need not be from the same source
• Office staples

- Handrail knobs and wire (optional)
- Paint/filler GWR Green – Railmatch, Ref: 2601
- Transfers – HMRS or Model Master
- Number plates – Narrow Planet or 247 Developments
- Coal
- Vacuum pipes (MJT or similar)
- Loco tools (Springside or similar)
- Loco crew.

Tools required:
- Scraper
- Knife
- Needle files
- Clamp
- Small nose pliers
- Side cutters
- Drills
- Brushes.

BODY MODIFICATIONS

Start by removing any unwanted mouldings from the body of the 48XX. Here on the donor body, the first thing to look at was the electrical cable running on the offside. A homemade scraper was used, consisting of an old triangular needle file ground down to a chisel point. A very sharp knife or a scalpel will do the same job, but watch those fingers and work very, very slowly. Note that the body has been clamped firmly to the bench to hold it still and to enable the free use of the other hand. The second similar job is the removal of the fireman's steps on the other side, as these were a later addition on most of the class.

The next possible removal is the cab-mounted whistle shield, which again was a later addition. On the model this is actually part of the roof moulding, but it is fairly easy to chop away and clean-up.

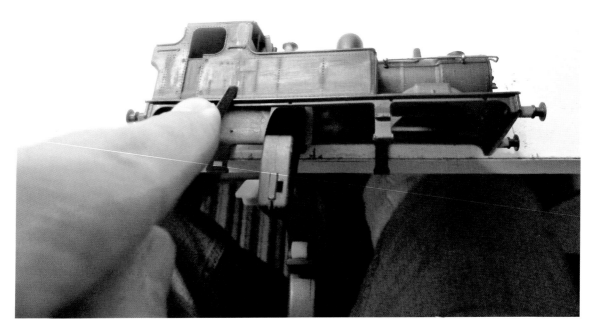

Removing the electrical cable mould with an old triangular needle file.

The bunker steps removed.

The whistle shield can be prised off and the roof edge cleaned up.

THE TOP FEED

The biggest job of the entire conversion is the possible removal of the top feed (the squarish lump behind the chimney). Top-feed equipment was only fitted to some of the class, so again you would need to check if your chosen loco was so fitted. The operation is a slow, careful job of cutting the plastic away one bit at a time with a pair of side cutters. When most of it has been removed, finish off with a flat needle file. Following that, clean off the adjoining pipework and, while you are at it, also the mould lines from the top of the boiler, which would need to go whether

The top-feed mould can be removed with side cutters and cleaned up with files.

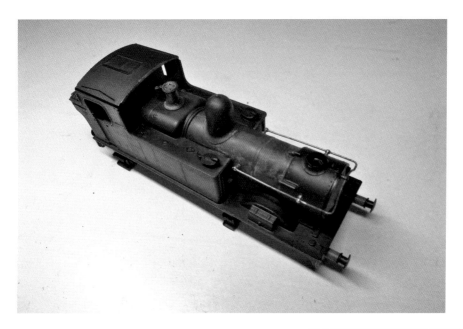

Top feed now completely removed, cleaned up and the boiler mould lines cleaned off.

you remove the top feed or not. Once these three operations have been carried out, the body will look a bit sorry for itself and should be given a wash and a preliminary coat of paint.

FIRE IRON HOOKS

One of the most obvious omissions from the model are the fire iron hooks which should be present on the rear of the bunker. White-metal or brass castings for these can be bought, but something slightly lower-tech will give an equally good visual result using a standard office staple bent to a reverse curve shape and inserted into 0.7mm holes. These holes should be drilled at 4mm and 11mm intervals from each edge, just below the line of horizontal rivets.

GLAZING

The model is not glazed and the rear spectacles are so obscured with the coal grilles that it hardly seems worth touching these. The front pair is much more obvious, so a few minutes and some clear plastic will do the job. The plastic used here is from the Wills building kits packs detailed later and this is perfect for this sort of job, as well as being essentially free. The measurements are 10mm high by a shade over 28mm wide with a top radius of

The fire iron hooks can be shaped from ordinary office staples.

The fire iron hooks are inserted into pre-drilled holes in the bunker.

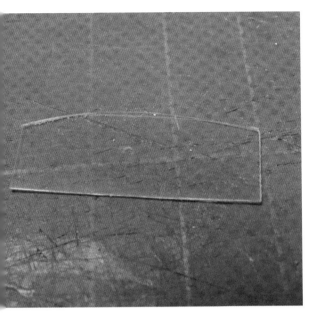

The cab glass can be shaped from a piece of packing plastic.

Cab glass fitted.

79mm. The best way to cut this is first to shape the radius on a larger piece, cut this roughly to size, then trial-fit and trim a little at a time until a good fit is obtained.

FINISHING OFF

Any final painting should now be carried out and your choice of lettering added. This particular example was to represent the first of the class in

Completed body painted and transfers and number plates added.

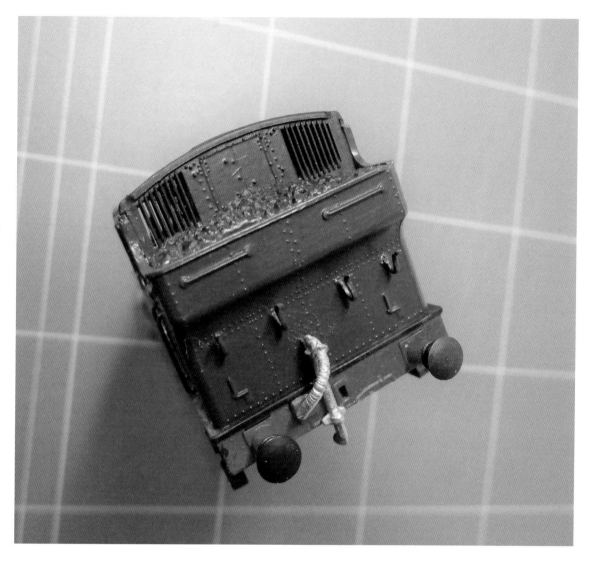

Vacuum pipes can be added from white-metal castings.

early condition, so etched-brass number plates purchased from Narrow Planet were stuck on with a drop of superglue and 'GREAT WESTERN' in full put on using 'pressfix' transfers from HMRS.

BUFFER BEAM DETAILS

The Airfix/Hornby body only has the auto-gear cover represented on the front buffer beam, but it is a work of minutes to add one at the rear using a 3mm square piece of 20thou plastic. New white-metal vacuum pipes can also be added, noting that in all photos of the class they are swung to the left when not in use.

Finally, add a crew (suitably cut away from the waist down to clear the motor) by sticking the figures to the inside of the cab doors. You should also add coal in the bunker and a set of lamps. These were mostly mounted as per stopping passenger train coding on top of the smokebox at the front and in a low central position at the rear, though some photos show the front lamp mounted centrally on the footplate for the same type of train. Any weathering can now be carried out as required, though being fairly new and mainly used on passenger duties they would have been quite well maintained in this respect and would

4800 complete with weathering, lamps and crew.

not be covered in the total filth that was a feature of the British Railways era machines.

The above alterations are just as applicable to any small GWR locomotive. Most of these had long careers and were nearly all rebuilt and/or modified along the way. It's just a case of picking your locomo-

tive, locating information and a photo or two, then working out what needs to be added or removed. Most RTR locomotives will benefit from a few basic additions and at the least a little light weathering and some coal and a crew.

CHAPTER SEVEN

MAIN BRANCH-LINE BUILDINGS

FIRST CONSIDERATIONS

When constructing a GWR branch layout, the size, shape and style of the buildings should be considered reasonably early on. Basic geography should be a factor with regard to specific building materials and, to some extent, the style of the architecture. There are, as usual, traps for the modeller to be wary of – standard buildings were indeed used in many places, but the branches were surprisingly wide-ranging in their building features. In short, it is very tricky to

spot a GWR branch-line station building if you take all of the other lineside features away. Much of this is due to the fact that the GWR did not actually own or run many of these branch lines to begin with. Add to that the element of cost for a locally financed line, and in most cases the use of local builders to complete the construction work and local building materials to reduce this cost where practical. The upshot of these factors was that there was much variation throughout the system, with no standard set of designs laid down from the outset.

Moreton-in-Marsh.
A standard GWR
station building.

The Cambrian influence. Ex-GWR station building at Devil's Bridge.

In later years, the GWR did build a number of what could loosely be called 'standard' buildings, which were constructed in the most on main lines and largely as replacements for earlier structures. The platform building pictured took the place of the original wooden station built by the Oxford, Worcester & Wolverhampton Railway and, although not on a branch line, is one of these standard type designs and can still be viewed today.

BUILDING MATERIALS AND DESIGN

Although some branch buildings were replaced (often due to increased traffic and track layout changes), many soldiered on throughout their existence with the same structures that had been built for the opening of the line. These were often constructed from local stone, or in many cases the cheaper option of timber-framed structures faced with timber boarding or corrugated iron sheet. For instance, the Cambrian Railways section often used the latter form of construction, giving a very 'light railway/agricultural' appearance and a long way from the company's Paddington station in both style and construction, as well as in mileage.

LOOK AT THE LOCALITY

As the buildings were so varied and hard to pin down, the modeller is free to improvise to some extent, so long as some basic colour rules are followed with regard to paintwork. A quick study of buildings in the locality of where you are to set your model will give you all the help that you'll need. If on the other hand you are modelling a prototype situation, all this work will have been done for you and it is just a case of obtaining drawings of the buildings concerned along with some photos. Or, if you are very lucky, if the buildings are still standing, you can make a site

The independent lines gave the GWR a varied look and could be very attractive. This building is at Chinnor.

Brunel's 'chalet' style building at Charlbury. A kit is available from Gaugemaster in 4mm scale.

visit with some suitable measuring equipment and a camera. The problem here is that the vast majority of the closed branch stations have been swept away under modern development, and those that are still open have been clouted with Western Region/ Railtrack cost-cutting and have been reduced, or knocked down and replaced with the ubiquitous bus shelters. Compared to other British railway companies, the GWR has suffered more than most in this respect. Although this is a negative aspect, the GWR modeller does benefit much more than any other company in that nearly everything has been documented photographically in books, on the Internet and in various museum collections. If you need the information, then someone out there has everything that you want.

The first project in this chapter is something to represent the heart of any passenger station layout – the actual station building.

PROJECT EIGHT: A SMALL KIT-BUILT STATION BUILDING

Small is the operative word here. Most novice modellers underestimate the room required for any aspect of a layout, but specifically the size of passenger station buildings, which even on branch lines could become quite extensive. We tend to think first of a single building with a couple of doors and windows in the front. They did exist in great numbers all over the system, but many were three times the length that we may imagine and contained several rooms, including office, parcels store, Ladies' waiting room, Gents' toilet, lamp room and so on. Something like this can soon take up 450mm of platform length in 4mm scale. Many modellers will be looking for something more compact and the trade serves us well with a large range of kits in the three major scales. The main readily available choices are from our old friends Ratio, Wills and Peco (which are all essentially the same company), but there are several smaller cottage industry type firms supplying models in card, plastic and wood, particularly in O gauge. These smaller ranges tend to come and go, so it's worth snapping something up quickly if you see it, whereas

Tip

When visiting model exhibitions look closely at the arrangement of buildings on the layouts. Do they follow the logical placement, or is there a subtle amount of freelancing? If the latter, decide if this would work for you, or does this offend by stretching reality too much?

the first three main ranges are plentiful and show no obvious sign of vanishing. These are all exclusively plastic kits, but if your preference is cardboard, the excellent Prototype Models range of GWR buildings is still available through Freestone Models.

On the same tack, there is now a growing range of downloadable card kits on the Internet. The overriding concern here is that the professional kit makers use a high-quality printing ink, which is more colourfast than that used in standard home printers. The colours of the latter have a tendency to fade, especially if the model is housed in a well-lit room.

The choice here for a first try at a building kit is the less commonly used Peco 'Manyways' building, which is produced in both brick and stone finishes. Alternative plastic kits would be the Wills small timber station, or the Ratio Models kit, which is closely based on Castle Cary station. The Wills kit is slightly smaller than the Peco product, while the Ratio kit is slightly larger. The Peco kit was chosen as the parts fit together very accurately and even with the couple of modifications described here, it is a very straightforward build.

Materials required:
• Peco Country Station Building, Ref LK 12
• Plastic strip 1mm
• Blu-tack
• Liquid solvent
• Paint
• Talcum powder.

Tip

The kit parts tend to have a little residue of the moulding release agent present, so it is well worth washing all the plastic parts in a bowl of warm water with a very tiny drop of washing-up liquid and allowing them to dry before you start.

Tools required:
- Craft knife
- Cutting mats
- Needle files/sanding stick
- Sheet-sanding board (homemade)
- Pin chuck and drills
- Brushes.

ADAPTING THE WALL SECTIONS

The prototype inspiration for this building was photos of Nelson station in the South Wales valleys. The station site has long gone under modern development and only very poor period photographs survive. None of these are of suitable quality to reproduce here, but can be viewed on the Internet (search: 'Nelson station Treharris'). The structure was a brick-built building with a simple roof line and a self-supporting canopy. Although it would need a completely scratch-built model to end up with something totally accurate, using an adapted Peco kit will certainly produce an acceptable representation.

MAIN WALLS

The first thing that needs to be done is to swap the ends around right for left, then cut a new window in what will now be the left-hand piece.

A new window can be marked out at a size of 17mm high × 12.5mm wide and can be drilled out using a drill in a pin chuck as shown, starting at the corners and drilling a line of holes on the inside of the mark line. Then simply join the holes with a knife and push the piece out. The hole can then be filed back to the lines. Finally, a new lintel can be cut from the sheet of glazing material, which is included in the kit, sized at 2 × 15mm and which can be added above the aperture level with the door.

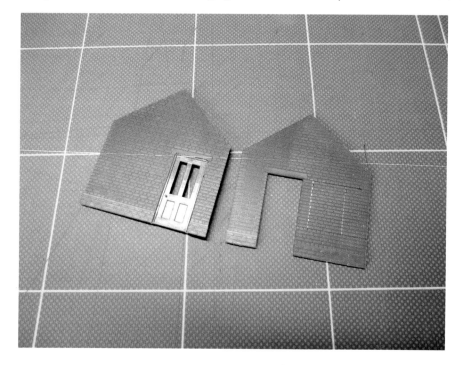

The door moved and the new window marked out in pencil.

*Drilling the aperture
for the new window.*

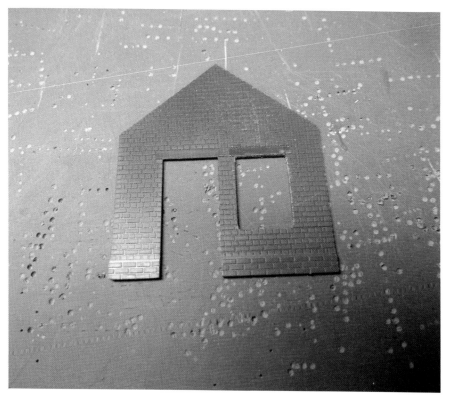

*The new lintel is
added above the
window using clear
plastic packing.*

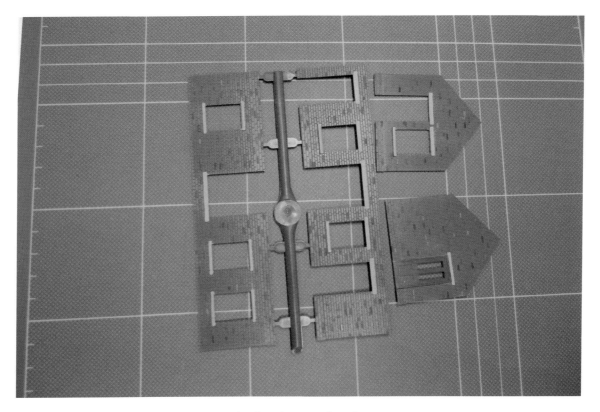

Windowsills are added, then these and the lintels are painted.

DETAILING THE PARTS

Most of the work involved to make this into a model that can be identified as a GWR station building is in the painting. The kit itself is very well made and if you just wanted to build it as per the instructions, it could probably be done in under an hour and you would still get the general flavour of a GWR station building. The task here is to make it alone tell the viewer that it is a Great Western building and most of that can be done with paint and a little extra detailing, giving the builder a model that not only achieves this, but creates a very individual building that will stand out from the others built from this kit. The first step is to add the windowsills and paint these and the lintels with 'light stone' (Humbrol 63 or similar). Then pick out random, but regular, bricks in dark grey and dark orange (67 and 62). This is far easier to achieve while the parts are still on the sprue and sitting flat on the work bench.

CONSTRUCTION

Drill the reference holes as indicated on the instructions. The walls can then be built up as pairs, checking that they are completely square. Most cutting mats will have grid lines to assist you with this. Alternatively, the square edge of a metal ruler can be used, or, better still, a small engineer's square. When all four walls are assembled, they can be given a wash of Light Grey (64), treating one wall at a time. Allow the paint to settle in the mortar joints and dry slightly, then 'flick' the paint off the brick surface with a tissue. This may take a couple of attempts to get the effect you want.

The card hallway can now be added, noting that the corners of the floor need to be removed to allow for the door frames. The windows should now be pre-painted white. This is over green plastic, so may need a couple of thin coats to cover adequately. When the paint is fully dry, fit the windows and doors to the building, using a minimal amount of solvent added from the rear.

One wall and one end are attached, making sure that all is totally square.

A base coat of brick is added and individual bricks picked out in red, orange and dark grey.

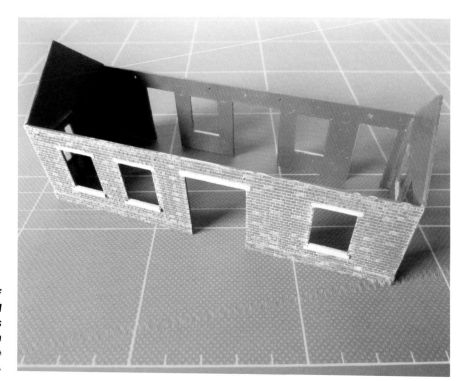

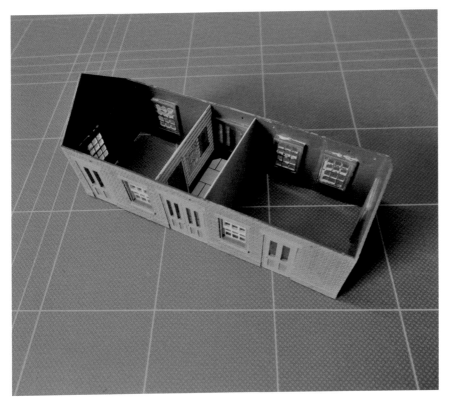

Windows and internal partitions are added.

THE ROOF AND A HOMEMADE TOOL

The roof comes in three parts. The narrower piece containing the moulded lettering is the front pitch. The moulds are quite thick at the edges, which does not represent the slate roofing very well. This can be improved by 'feathering'. This involves sanding the edge at approximately 45 degrees to give a final appearance of something much thinner. A simple sanding board can be quickly made using a flat offcut of MDF or chipboard, with a piece of sandpaper of around 150mm square stuck firmly and smoothly to it. The 45-degree angle is made by gently rubbing the roof moulding forward and back, checking after each couple of strokes. Be careful not to remove any material from the overall length. This technique will be used extensively in the scratch-building section of this chapter. Again, a few minutes of practice with some scrap plastic is time well spent.

When all the lower and end edges have been feathered, loosely fit the two main parts to the building and attach temporarily with small pieces of

The roof sections have their edges 'feathered' using a homemade sanding board.

Painting Tips

Only a relatively small number of colours are used for this building and all are Humbrol acrylics, which are available from many model and toy shops:

- 27 Sea Grey
- 33 Black
- 34 White
- 62 Leather (dark orange)
- 63 Sand
- 64 Light Grey
- 67 Tank Grey
- 70 Brick Red.

The GWR colours were defined into three base colours: light stone; mid-stone; and dark stone. Here, 63 has been used neat as the light stone, and a 50/50 mix of 70 and 63 for the mid-stone used around the window frames and the doors.

The photograph here shows a shelter at Didcot Museum, which clearly illustrates the official suggested painting style. It should, however, be noted that this would have been affected by local variations, sunlight and general weathering, so does not need to be stuck to rigidly, although it does need to be at the very least suggested in order to get the right GWR feel.

Mortar Washes
Mortar washes can be used to create weathering effects or to fill mortar joints. Simply add paint to the brush, quickly dip into water and draw across the face of the model. The paint will dilute and run across the surface of the model, coating it with the thin film and settling in the joints. Any run-off can be picked up with the tip of the brush. Practise this on some scrap wall material before you attempt it on the model proper.

This shelter at Didcot Railway Centre shows the recommended paint colours.

The roof sections are held together using Blu-tack to assist.

Blu-tack. Line up the ridge join between these two and run solvent along it; but do not fix these to the main structure yet, as you are essentially using the walls purely as a jig. When this assembly has set, add the ridge piece. The roof section can now be lifted off and painted away from the rest of the building.

Paint the built roof section with an overall coat of Tank Grey (67), then pick out a few single slates in lighter or darker shades by mixing a small amount of the dark grey with a drop of white or black on a piece of scrap plastic or card. While the roof section is drying, give the internal walls of the main structure a rough coat of black to kill the light reflection inside the building; that is, unless you wish to add any internal detail which needs to be seen clearly, or if you should desire to add any internal lighting.

SECONDARY FITTINGS

Barge Boards

Fit the roof by adding solvent to the joins on the *inside* of the building. When firm, the barge boards can be added. These can now be pushed right up to the feathered edges of the roof line and fixed using a thin card spacer to obtain a consistent gap between the barge board and the wall. Note that the barge boards are 'handed', so check that you have unmatched pairs for each end and that they are the right way around before final fixing. As a final touch, a finial can be added using 1mm strip plastic or card 7mm long and which has been cut to a V at each end. This covers the join in the bargeboards and also replicates those on the building at Nelson. Then paint any remaining door and window units and add the glazing.

A Flat Canopy

Many GWR station buildings had an almost flat, self-supporting platform canopy without any platform posts and getting something close to this drastically alters the look of the finished kit.

Add the saw-tooth canopy edge to the underside front. The moulding is very bendy, so work your way along at about 10mm at a time to try to get it as straight as possible. From the second shortest piece on the sprue, cut two smaller pieces to match the length of the ends and fix to the roof in the same way. Then to represent the lead roof, add four 0.5mm strips of plastic or card at 25mm intervals on the top

The barge boards are fitted using a card spacer to keep them consistent and to stop them sagging while the solvent cures.

Finials can be added from lengths of plastic strip.

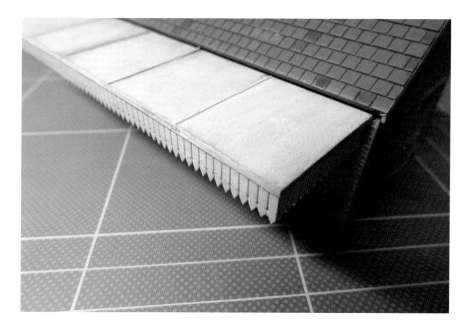

More plastic strip is used to simulate jointing on the canopy roof. This roof tucks under the main section.

Tip

As with the window units, it is best to pre-paint the secondary fittings with at least one coat while they are still on the sprue. This not only gives you a handle with which to move them around, but also negates any problems with getting the fitting colours on the pre-painted brickwork.

of the canopy, then paint the entire roof Light Grey (64). When fully dry, add a thin wash of dark grey and possibly a second very subtle wash of green. When you are happy with your work and all the paint is dry, add the canopy to the front of the building and the gutter piece to the rear. Also add the down pipes at the front and rear at this point.

Chimney

The chimney can now be made up and the brickwork treated as per the main walls. The pots should be painted Matt Leather (62) and the top plate a 50/50 mix of Sand (63) and Light Grey (64) to represent a concrete or cement material. Add the chimney

Flashing can be added using thin paper soaked in plastic solvent.

*The completed
station building.*

*This building at
Llanuchwllyn could
be constructed using
the Dapol (ex-Airfix)
booking hall kit as a
base to work from.*

The station building at New Radnor would make an excellent prototype for a compact layout.

assembly in place on the roof and let it set. Then as an extra bit of detailing add some lead flashing around the joint. Cut a 1.5mm strip of thin paper (a magazine was used here) and add it carefully to the foot of the chimney using solvent, then pressing lightly with the back of a knife blade to bed it in. Don't be tempted to use your fingertips. Paint this with a mix of light and dark grey. Finally, when all the paint is virtually dry, use a large flat brush to add a dusting of talcum powder over the whole roof, working it into the joints to tone down the stark grey.

PROJECT NINE: BRANCH SIGNAL BOX

WHAT TYPE OF SIGNAL BOX?

Out of all the likely branch station buildings, the signal box is probably the trickiest to construct. The lower floor is straightforward enough, but the open upper floor will need careful consideration; the space inside looks odd if it is not filled with something and there is no way to dodge around this unless you

model it 'switched out' and boarded up. There are other options, of course. With regard to small branch termini, not all had a large standard style signal box – many used only a small hut enclosing the few levers, with a window giving visibility along the line.

A lot of stations had no box at all, making do with an open ground frame locked with the line token for the main points and local point levers for the secondary throws such as sidings. The starting signal would also be operated from the frame, or possibly separately as per Ashburton, where the Station Master operated the station's starter signal via a lever set on the platform. A small signal 'hut' would not be hard to scratch-build and a good starting point would be the example at Watlington, drawings for which are available from the trade. Likewise, an open ground frame is easily made from scratch, or alternatively a plastic kit is available from Ratio Models in 4mm scale. As usual, most of these choices are down to personal preference and a study of prototype photos. There is also the aspect of train operation, as of course signal boxes are inextricably linked to this, with their size

Most GWR signal boxes have now been demolished. This example still stands, though boarded up and in use as a permanent way team office at Pwlleli.

and shape dictated by track layouts and traffic flows, and to some extent the box and all these operational aspects should be considered as a whole during the initial planning process.

STANDARD BOX OR INDEPENDENT BUILDER?

The GWR did build its own standard design boxes and did replace some units that were installed by the absorbed lines. However, the sleepy branch line beloved of many modellers would probably be fairly low on the list and would be left with original equipment unless there was a problem with maintenance or if the traffic changed, requiring the track, signalling and box to be altered. One of the easiest ways to reproduce a small branch box in 4mm scale is to use the kits produced by Ratio Models. One of its products is of a large main-line type box, but the other two are very suitable for our subject and are both based on the box at Highley on the Severn Valley Railway. The smallest 'platform-mounted' kit is just a cut-down version of the larger. The proto-

type box was supplied to the Severn Valley Railway Company (later the West Midland Railway and later still the GWR) by Makenzie and Holland, who, along with Saxby and Farmer, furnished many of the pre-Grouping railway companies with signalling equipment. Therefore, it is perfect for any branch model. This can also visually be its downfall, as the

Tip

Club sales stands at exhibitions are a good source of second-hand, but untouched, building kits. These are often initially purchased for a specific project that does not materialize, and are subsequently sold on. They do need a quick check over to see if they look complete, but even if they're not, they can be a good supply of windows and doors if they are cheap enough. The kit used here came from such a source.

The original 1883 Mackenzie and Holland Type 3 signal box at Highley is the prototype inspiration for the 4mm scale Ratio kit.

same kit is used over and over on many layouts and is rarely adapted from the basic kit instructions. This next project discusses the building of the kit, suggests a few small modifications and an effective budget approach to the interior along the way.

Materials required:
• Ratio Models platform/ground-mounted signal box, Ref: 503
• Wills brick sheet
• 20 × 10thou strip
• 1mm micro rod
• 30thou sheet (scrap)
• 60thou sheet (optional)
• Various scrap plastic.
• Liquid solvent
• Paint.

Tools required:
• As per the previous station building project.

LOWER FLOOR

The walling for the lower floor as supplied is of a stone type. This may be just what you need for a box set in Cornwall or another south-west line, but what if your branch is in the West Midlands or Wales? One way of quickly personalizing the Ratio box is to replace the stone with brick sheet. This is simply a case of measuring the existing parts and replicating them using Wills sheet, so there is a need to detail the operation here, it is also possible to increase or decrease the height should you wish. The new parts can be set around the floor as shown.

The other possibility is to add a very small window, or windows, at the front. The area inside is

The base of the Ratio kit is replaced with brick parts by simply copying the original stone pieces.

The stone chimney stack part at the rear is also replaced with Wills brick sheet.

the interlocking room – though 'room' is stretching the description somewhat. The link equipment inside would likely be accessed through the floor of the box on a building of this size, but adding a small window to give a tiny amount of light would give the plain brickwork some visual relief.

UPPER SECTION

The upper walls can now be constructed, noting that the stone chimney breast has also had its part replaced with brick sheet. Of course, if your box has its rear wall against the layout's backscene and is not visible, you need not bother with this extra part. This section of the kit's construction is by far the most difficult and careful note should be taken of the arrangement of the window frames detailed in the kit's instruction sheet. The painting of this upper section is best carried out at this point, as it is easier to handle without the roof and lower sections attached.

INSIDE

As mentioned above, a signal box without any interior details looks extremely odd. Full detailing kits are available and some modellers take this to

extremes by adding everything including the cat and teacups, often arranging for the roof to be removable so that this is fully visible. Without going to this detail level, a middle ground can be taken. The box will look glaringly empty with nothing, but once the glazing is added and the roof is on, it's quite hard to distinguish any exact details. Provided that enough recognizable visual information is included, the eye is fooled into thinking that there is more going on than is actually the case.

First to be tackled is the line equipment. This is usually mounted in one of two ways: either suspended from the ceiling using metal struts, or on a wooden 'bridge'. An Internet image search of signal box interiors will provide you with ample photographic inspiration for this. Here, a simple bridge has been constructed with throwaway items – mainly sprue from the kit itself. It does not need to be highly detailed – unless you want to do this. A series of rough shapes is more than adequate to give an impression.

LEVER FRAME

The lever frame is another simple dodge. A piece of 60thou sheet should be cut to size and shaped into the form of a gentle curve using a sanding stick.

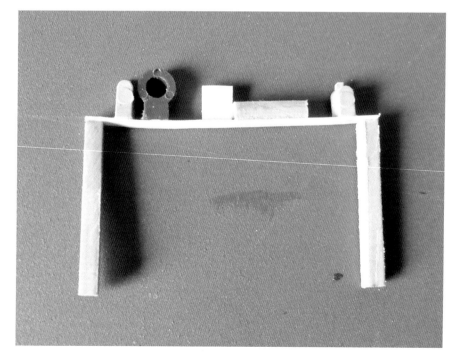

An instrument bridge can be made cheaply from offcuts of sprue.

The interior of the box at Highly. Note the struts supporting the bridge and the signal diagram above; also the human touches such as the sofa.

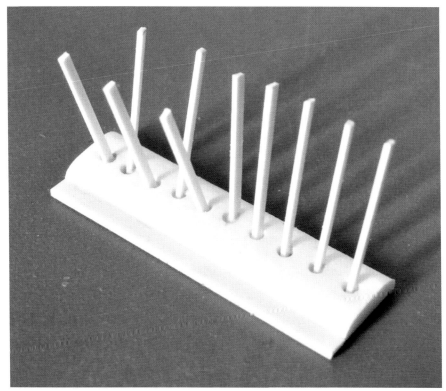

The lever frame can be made from plastic sheet and strip.

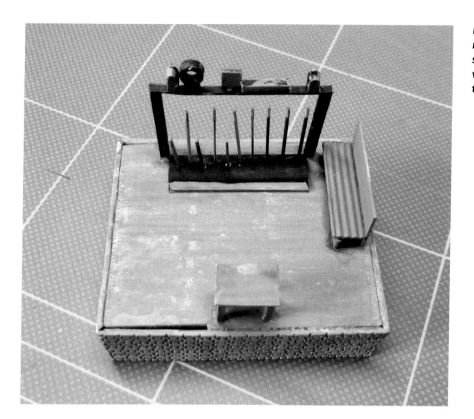

Even a quite crude representation looks surprisingly realistic when contained in the box.

A kickplate from 30thou sheet can be added along the leading edge. Holes of around 1.5mm diameter can be drilled along the plastic at around 2–3mm intervals and lengths of 20 × 10thou strip added at various angles as shown. This whole arrangement should reflect your layout's track and signal plan, but ten to fifteen is probably about right for most boxes of this size. Remember that 'spares' were usually put in to allow for any future track or signalling changes.

The bridge and lever frame can now be painted. The bridge will require a coat of sloppy brown, the frame a glossy black and the levers the colours to match your track layout. The basic colours are as follows: signal levers – red; point levers – black and facing point lock levers – blue. Depending on your time period, distant signal levers would be green and later yellow. These are just basic colours, but they should suffice for most branch applications. The tip (handles) of the lever can be painted a pale grey or silver. Admittedly this is all fairly crude, but it is surprising how good this will look in the finished box without having to add reams of

expensive detail. Any other items can be added now; here, a simple table and a bench have been built from scrap plastic; again just crude shapes.

THE ROOF SECTION

The roof can now be built up as per the kit instructions. The only addition here is the application of some thin paper strips around the base of the chimney to simulate lead flashing, which has been described in the station building project. The roof is best painted separately to avoid damage and to keep the brown paint way from the cream on the woodwork of the upper floor. The usual 'GWR stone' colours can be used, but here the feel required was for an original company's colours to still be in use after the GWR had taken over.

STEPS AND BALCONY

The set of steps and balcony parts that come with the smaller Ratio Models kit include those that are included in the larger. It is therefore possible with

The roof parts are constructed as a separate item. Some modellers often leave this loose so as to be able to detail and view the inside.

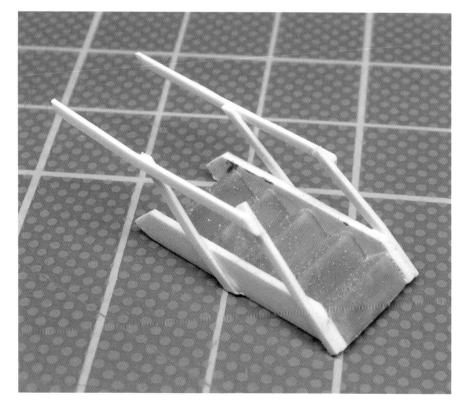

New lighter timber steps can be made using the kit parts combined with plastic sheet and strip.

A new balcony section can be made from the spare parts in the kit. Note the offset opening.

the addition of a little bit of plastic strip to make up a narrow balcony and wooden steps, which will give a lighter feel than the designed stone steps.

The first thing to do is to take the step moulding and edge it with some 30thou plastic sheet – 4mm deep. The ends are very much done by eye. The lower uprights (nearest the camera) are from 20 × 10thou again, are 14mm high and should have a little left at the top as a suggestion of a finial. The set in the middle are 13mm high. The handrails should match the angle of the side boards, but leave them over long at the top end until the final fitting.

The balcony floor used the part in the kit cut down lengthways to four planks wide. The handrails are a trial and error arrangement of parts, starting with the largest part and working outward. Having the steps slightly offset to the door creates a more interesting view than just straight up and in. Steps were often arranged this way to prevent the signalman walking out of the door and falling down the steps. This whole design and shape is not unlike the smaller box that used to stand at Dolgellau on

Tip

To be borne in mind in conjunction with the last tip, it is worth picking up old out of print line history books on the GWR. These days they have often been superseded by something glossier, but the raw information is still there and can be very valuable. Many of the older books also contain building drawings that you can both copy and learn a lot from. Many of the original Oakwood Press titles and the Bradford Barton picture albums can often be found dirt cheap at exhibitions and make it worthwhile purchasing even if they only contain a couple of useful photos. Working on a 50p per useful photo ratio to the price is a good rule of thumb for purchases.

The box from Barmouth Station is a small 'type 1' design built by Dutton & Co. for the Cambrian Railways in 1890 and now stands on the Llangollen Railway. In common with many boxes, it has a small porch jettied out from the doorway.

The completed Ratio signal box.

the Cambrian line, though in mirror image to this. The extended balcony is for the signalman to stand to receive, and hand out, the line token to passing locomotive drivers and could in reality extend even further forward should you wish.

FINAL DETAILS

At this point, the details such as fire buckets and the lamp can be added and the roof fixed on along with the step assembly. Lastly, a name board should be fitted at the front.

The Ratio kit is highly adaptable and can be viewed, like most building kits, as a set of parts ripe for adaptation. The big plus is that it gives you the upper floor, which is otherwise tricky to scratch-build; all the other sections can be adapted to suit your layout.

While the Ratio kit is a cut-down version of the Highley box, it would be possible to do the opposite and extend it downward as per this box mounted on the embankment at Bewdley. Such conversions would pull what is a fairly standard item away from the commonplace.

GOODS SHEDS – SOME DESIGN CONSIDERATIONS

Most modellers of any persuasion want a goods shed on the layout and those modelling the GWR are not any different. In prototype terms there are many varied sheds to choose from, though we tend to think first in terms of the typical 'large over the track' type. Again, this is as much to do with what we have seen on other people's layouts and what the model trade supplies, as anything else. The first bubble to burst is that not every branch station had a goods shed; it very much depended on the type and amount of traffic handled on the line, as the company would not have been keen to spend money putting up a large building for no reason. Therefore, if the main traffics, such as coal, could be 'open transferred', no shed would be needed.

Where goods sheds – which were more usually called warehouses by the GWR – did exist, they would not only reflect the traffic flows, but local architecture styling and building materials as well. The GWR did build what could be loosely described as a standard shed, but most branch sheds were partly designed locally and showed a great variety of approaches. The trade provides several kits for the GWR modeller: Ratio and Wills produce plastic kits, while Superquick and Prototype Models offer some very suitable card models. If card is to your liking, there are an increasing number of 'download/print at home' shed kits available on the Internet at very low prices in 2, 4 and 7mm scales. There are also resin goods sheds available ready to plant from both Bachmann and Hornby for 2 and 4mm scales.

There are two ways of approaching this: either decide what sort of shed (if any) that your layout requires, then see if you can use or adapt a commercial item; or take a commercially produced kit or moulding and plan around it. Thirdly, you can research a prototype building, start from scratch and build it yourself.

The goods shed at Ashburton clearly showing its broad-gauge roots.

The much extended goods shed at Moretonhampstead.

THE BROAD-GAUGE ASPECT

One of the larger over-track designs is still standing at Ashburton. Originally built by the Buckfastleigh, Totnes & South Devon Railway, it is now in retail use and is what most modellers think of when planning a goods shed on their layout. As can be seen, the problem can be one of baseboard space – a goods shed in floor-plan terms is essentially 50 per cent non-railway and these larger over-track designs can be very space-hungry on the baseboard. The shed was designed to keep goods clean and dry until they could be transferred, hence the large platform/storage area. To make matters worse in model layout space terms, the Ashburton example in particular is built to broad-gauge measurements, indicated by the wide doorway over the track. This may be exactly the feel that you want, as it points directly back to a broad-gauge period branch construction, but a similar shed in 4mm scale would need somewhere in the region of 180mm square of baseboard area, which is not always available on a small layout.

LESS OBVIOUS ALTERNATIVES

If you are short of baseboard space, there are alternatives. Smaller sheds existed all over the system – several to a basic design by William Clarke. The example below is at Llanuwchllyn on the (now) 60cm narrow-gauge Bala Lake preservation railway, which runs on the old GWR standard-gauge trackbed. The shed at this location is easily accessible should you wish to examine it or obtain measurements. There is another similar building still standing at Portesham in Dorset, though on private land. As can be seen the shed stood next to the line, rather than over it, giving the modeller a chance to have a more open feel to the goods yard. The approximate prototype floor plan is 7,620mm × 4,115mm (25 × 13½ft).

An interesting halfway point between these two designs is where the road access entered the shed at ground level, whereas the rail traffic was loaded from outside through a side door often covered by a small canopy, as with the shed at New Radnor. This is also very accessible, but stands within the boundaries of a caravan site, so a polite request for permission to view is required.

If the traffic was very light, goods inward were often handled and held in a lock-up store on the branch station platform itself, often using one of the GWR's 'pagoda' buildings, which are discussed in a later chapter.

The small shed at Llanuchwllyn, now used by the Bala Lake Railway.

The hybrid design shed at New Radnor with the rail access outside and road access inside.

1446 shunts the station at Hemyock in 1959. In the background stands a standard corrugated shed, which is the basis for this project. MICHAEL FARR

PROJECT TEN: A SMALL GOODS WAREHOUSE

The final building in this chapter covers a goods shed that will fit just about anywhere on the GWR system, but yet while being quite typical, is not what most people would first think of as being a classic GWR design. The original wooden goods shed at Hemyock on the Culm Valley line was knocked down in 1932 to allow for an expanded track arrangement and a new shed was built a few hundred yards away on a loop line. This new shed was constructed from corrugated iron and asbestos sheeting over a timber frame and mounted on a timber platform. The inside of the shed was accessed by two large sliding doors hung from long, deep metal plates. It was, in short, a cheap option to cope with the non-dairy traffic handled at the station and was representative of the GWR's small building policy in the early part of the twentieth century.

Tip

There are a few simple rules: the old adage 'measure twice, cut once' holds true and working slowly through the instructions will ensure that you get a building that will be as good as most commercial plastic kits.

A model of this goods shed can be scratch-built in 4mm scale using two to three packs of Wills building sheets and a single sheet of plain plastic sheet. The modelling techniques used are similar to those employed in the changes made to the station building covered earlier – if you can build that, you can cope with this. The build detailed below is not an exact replica, but a building which is inspired by the prototype, while taking into consideration that this may be the reader's first piece of scratch-building. Close-up prototype photos are available in Paul Karau's *Great Western Branch Line Termini*, *The Culm Valley Light Railway* by the Oakwood Press and of course on the Internet.

Materials required:
• Wills corrugated sheet SSMP 216
• Wills Flemish bond building sheet SSMP 226 (optional)
• Wills building pack A SS46
• A small amount of 30thou plastic sheet
• Solvent
• Paint.

Tools required:
• Cutting mat
• Steel ruler
• Craft knife
• Engineer's square (optional)
• Needle files and sanding stick
• Sanding board
• Brushes.

CUTTING AND MARKING OUT THE SIDES

The real shed made use of full-length pieces of corrugated iron so the sides are a fairly predetermined 96mm long by 35mm high. The first thing to do is to cut one side from one Wills sheet.

First, orientate the sheet so that the iron sheeting overlaps are working downward. Then turn the sheet over. The maker's name, if it is present, should oddly now be upside down. To help you, mark a large 'T' for 'top' on the appropriate edge (keep doing this all the way though the cutting processes). To get the full sheet appearance on the model, the lower 14mm needs to be removed. Mark 14mm up from the bottom, draw a pencil line, and, using a new blade and a steel ruler, make a series of light cuts along the line. Don't try to cut right through yet. Instead, after three or four cuts, bend the sheet so that the cut opens up, *but do not be tempted to snap it*. The sheet should then be able to be cut through in one final knife movement.

Clean up the edge and mark as per the illustration, 96mm from the right-hand end and 35mm from the bottom. Cut the long horizontal line first, followed by the short vertical line. Clean the part up and put

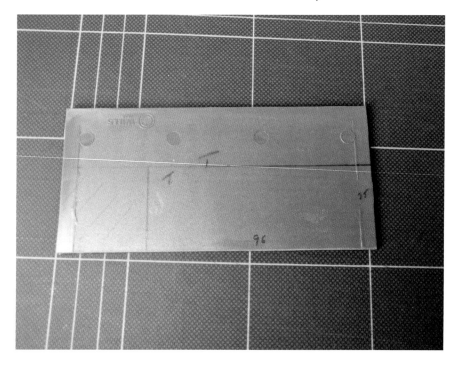

The wall section is marked out on the rear of the sheet. Notice the orientation of the Wills stamp. With this upside down, the sheet will be the right way up.

The edges are mitred by using the sanding board as per the station building roof treated earlier. The angle needs to be just a shade under 45 degrees.

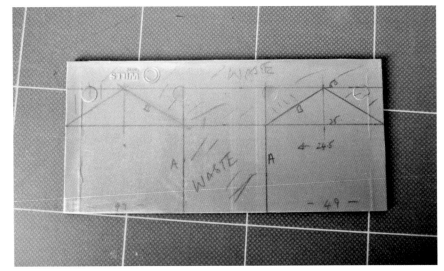

The ends marked out. Keep the triangular waste pieces for corner supports.

the waste pieces aside for use on another project. Repeat this whole process for the second side on a new sheet.

MITRED EDGES

Both parts need to be mitred at each end to a shade under 45 degrees. Also, and just as important, the upper top edge needs to be mitred at the front for its entire length. This is so that the roof pieces only sit on the *inner* edge of the sides. All the mitre work should be done using a homemade sanding board as described during the station building roof section above.

THE ENDS

The ends should be marked out as follows: orientate the sheet and remove the lower 14mm as before. Clean the edge and mark a new horizontal line 50mm from the bottom, followed by a second parallel line at 35mm from the bottom. Then mark the widths at 49mm from each edge and draw vertical lines upward. Find the centre of each end at 24.5mm and mark where this intersects with the 50mm horizontal line. Mark the angled roof lines from the edges and from the 49mm lines to this point as shown. You should end up with something similar to the illustration. Before you cut anything, double check all your measurements – you don't get a second chance.

Tip

When marking plastic sheet, use a pencil of the propelling type rather than the wood type. This will stay sharp and give a clean fine line all the way through the marking-up process. What you don't want is a thick messy line that can quickly lose you a couple of millimetres when you try to establish the cut line.

Remove the waste section above the 50mm line, followed by the vertical lines marked 'A'. Then follow this with the angled lines marked 'B'. This should leave you with four triangular pieces. These are to be used later, so don't discard them. Clean all the parts and mitre the edges (but not the tops) as before.

ASSEMBLING THE WALLS

Add one end to one side using solvent applied to the inside of the joint. The use of an engineer's square is recommended here, but is not essential. The markings on the cutting mat will work just as well. Make sure that the two parts are vertical as well as square on the joint. Have a dry run first and if the parts don't give a clean joint at the outside edge, remove a little more material on the mitre until they do. Add the other end in similar fashion and use the waste triangles from cutting the ends to reinforce the corners. Wills do produce small corner joiners to do the same job, but for something as invisible as this, using waste sheet is far more economical. When these three parts have set firmly, add the second side piece.

ROOF PARTS

Take a third piece of Wills sheet and treat as before by removing the lower section. Then mark a line 99mm from one side and remove the waste. Then mark a line 31mm down and remove. However, before you do any of this, make sure that 99mm and 31mm will cover a) the width of your structure; and b) the depth of the angled sections from the peak to a few millimetres past the side walls. Getting something which works as a whole is better than blindly

Ends and one side fixed showing 'waste' corner supports.

Roof section marking out.

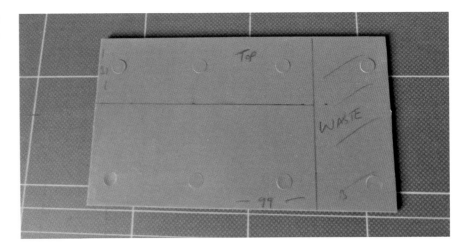

The edges are first 'feathered', then the bottom edge is worked with a rat-tail file.

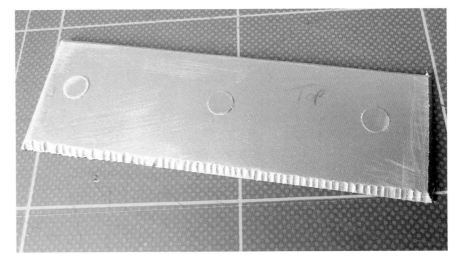

sticking to the roof measurements given here. If the size of your walls has wobbled slightly, no one will notice. If the roof doesn't fit, everyone will. So adjust if necessary and repeat with a second piece.

As with the station building above, the roof pieces benefit from being thinned down at the edges. This should now be done on both parts, keeping the angle fairly shallow. The top edges where the two parts meet at the ridge should be sanded down to around a 35-degree angle, so that they will meet with a sharp edge. A little trial and error is needed here to get a good fit. Finally, the lower edge should also be sanded down as per the edges and followed up with a series of notches made with a round (rat-tail) needle file. This gives the impression of the thin edge and the corrugations of the sheeting.

The roof pieces can now be added to the main structure. As before, use Blu-tack to hold the parts until you are completely satisfied. When they are attached, cut a strip of ordinary copy paper 5mm wide, pre-fold it along the centre using the edge of a table or similar as a former and add to the roof by flooding the paper with solvent. Firm down with the back of the brush that you are using. As always, *do not use your fingers* as you are likely to end up with your fingerprints etched into the plastic and the whole roof will be wasted. The entire structure should be painted light stone if you want to stick to GWR colours, though there seems to be a fairly wide choice of painting styles, with a coat of black bitumen being common. That is the basic structure finished, then it's on to the outward decoration.

With the roof on, a paper ridge piece is added with solvent. Do not smooth down with your fingers.

Planking can be formed by drawing the knife sideways against a ruler, creating a scribed 'V'.

Tip

When scribing parts, leave the part attached to the sheet rather than cutting it out first. This gives you plenty of sheet to hang on to and reduces the chance of slippage.

DOORS

Using a sheet of 30thou plastic, mark out a door 24mm wide by 27mm high. Mark the top plate with a horizontal line 2mm from the top, then add vertical plank marks at 2mm intervals. When you are happy with this, scribe the marks with two or three strokes using the knife point held at a right angle as shown.

RUNNING PLATE

Using the same sheet, cut a strip 3mm wide and 58mm long for the door running plate, followed by two smaller strips 1mm wide and around 15mm

Door hangers from strip and the rail from 30thou sheet. Note the spacing blocks.

The complete door assembly.

long. These are for the hanger plates, are over-length and can be trimmed down later. Add these to the door as shown and also add spacer pieces from scrap sheet to the rear of all parts. These will hold the door a couple of scale inches away from the wall.

Add the running plate to the door 1.5mm from the left-hand end. Then make up wheels by cutting a 3mm-wide strip, rounding off the ends so that it resembles a short lolly stick. Trim these ends off and round the final part of the disc. This is a bit of a fiddle and if you can find something of a similar disc nature in your scrap box or even tiny washers, so much the better. Add the discs to the top of the hanging plates and trim the length. Paint the whole assembly in a GWR mid-stone colour using Humbrol 63 and 70 mixed 50/50, then put the assembly to one side. If the building is to be viewed from all sides, repeat the entire exercise for the second door on the other side. If not, you can move on. If there are to be two doors, it would be worth making all the parts as pairs on the sheet to start with to save marking-out time.

GUTTERS AND FACIA

Cut two strips of 30thou sheet 3mm wide and 99mm long to match the roof length. Paint these mid-stone colour and add to the walls front and back tight under the roof line.

Using three gutter pieces from the Wills building pack, mark on which side the actual gutter is, then make a light knife cut directly above this. Using this as a guide, run the point of a round needle file down and ream out the gutter. It is best to work from the centre to each end – doing the opposite is likely to result in the file snagging; the thin plastic will then fold up like a concertina, followed by a trip to the waste bin.

Cut the pieces off the sprue and remove about 1.5mm from the flat rear of the gutter to line it up with the roof edge. Using one, butt-join shorter sections to the others to make two full-length gutters. Paint the gutters mid-stone and run black paint into the channel. Then add these to the already fitted facia boards below the roof, lining the channel up with the roof lower edge.

Wills gutters can be opened up with a rat-tail needle file.

The brick base. Note the mitre joins.

The completed shed.

Similar designs were used all over the GWR. This is a platform lamp hut version at Bodmin.

These designs are also still in service on the main line, for example this end-window version at St Erth in Cornwall.

PLATFORM

The Hemyock shed is mounted on a timber platform, which in turn is supported on a series of X-frame timbers. While this is by no means impossible to make, the novice scratch-builder may find it easier to add a solid base from brick or stone sheet. Here the decision was to use Wills Flemish brick sheet. The measurements are 10mm high strips (or seven brick courses if you prefer), with probable lengths of 94mm and 47mm. These should be mitred as usual and constructed separately. Note that the base should sit just inside the edge of the corrugated sheeting all the way around. This is so that the rain would run off the iron sheeting and not settle at the bottom, causing decay.

FINISHING OFF

The door assemblies can now be added, making sure that the door is central. Drainpipes from the Wills building pack can also be added front and back and any further painting and weathering carried out.

This is quite a simple structure, but it should get you used to working with plastic sheet and hopefully will inspire you to try more complex subjects. This basic design was reasonably common on the system in various guises and with detail differences. A few are even now still being used, both on preserved lines and on the public main lines.

CHAPTER EIGHT

GWR SIGNALS

WHY SIGNALS?

It has often been remarked that the difference between a train set and a model of a railway is the presence of signals on the layout; and in very general terms it is the image of the red semaphore signal which says 'railway' more than the actual trains. In some ways this is understandable, not only in image terms but in reality, once you grasp that except in only a few cases, the signals will happily work without the trains, but the trains will not work without the signals. If no signals are present to control operations, the trains will sooner or later bump into each other with quite catastrophic results.

The use of fixed mechanical signals developed in parallel with the railways; before this, trains had been controlled by flag men at certain points. However, as traffic grew, this method became unworkable and systems were developed for keeping trains running on the same line, but at a safe distance apart. This historical development is a highly complex one, with a gradual improvement in mechanics and, in later years, electric control. To describe this in detail would be outside of the scope of this book, but there are other volumes that deal exclusively with the subject. What is relevant here is a short discussion on how a model of a branch line may be signalled.

BRANCH SIGNALLING

The signals on a typical single-track branch line do one of three things. Firstly, they prevent trains colliding by controlling the entry to a stretch of track known as a section. This means that once a train has entered this section, a signal that indicates stop will immediately be set to 'on' to prevent another train from following, until the first train is clear of that

Short board starter signal and shunt arm.

'Sighting boards' were often used if the signal was against a dark background such as a bridge.

particular section. Secondly, signals prevent a train running into an object that blocks the train's path, for instance a closed level crossing gate or points that are set against the train. Thirdly, there are signals that give an advanced warning on how the next signal is set (known as distant signals), so that the driver can prepare to slow and stop. This outline simplifies the system somewhat, but once this set of basic rules is understood it becomes easy to fill in any variations and detail.

The other thing for the branch-line modeller to understand is the prototype distances involved between the signals. This generally means that unless you are able to model great lengths of open line, the number of signals outside of individual station limits are likely to be few; and in most cases distant signals will not be needed on the average size layout.

OTHER SIGNALLING FACTORS

It is also worth considering branch-line traffic levels. If a branch is built with double track it will naturally need more signal control than a single track. Rarely do the lines on a double-track line not converge at some point; this is usually around station passing loops. Conversely, some branch lines were built with greatly reduced speed limits and minimal signalling – this was the case with the several 'light railways' that the GWR absorbed, or which came under the GWR's control at the 1923 Grouping. An open stretch of line can be very lightly controlled, but the trackwork within station limits can be intensely signalled and the GWR was renowned for over-signalling in this situation.

The good news is that the classic simple branch terminus model may only require one semaphore signal arm; so less for you to build. The bad news is that any signals that are required are best planned into the layout from the start. If you build a terminus station with a single platform and a rapidly approached exit under a bridge, as many layouts are, all that may be required is a simple 'starter' signal – one board (arm) on a post at the end of the platform. This board 'starts' the train and allows entry from the closed area of the station into the first section of open line. The corresponding signal is the 'home' signal, which does the same thing from the other direction and controls entry from the open section into the station. Most people will have sat on a stationary train waiting to get into a city station just outside the limits, being held at a home signal until a platform is free to take the train. On a model with a close scenic exit under a bridge, this home signal can be conveniently omitted, as it is 'off scene'.

In the station proper there can be a number of smaller arms controlling entry and exit from sidings or other areas and in some cases these allow the engine to pass the starter signal even if it is set

Shunt signals and calling-on arms could often be mounted on a separate bracket.

Shunt signals and calling-on arms could also be mounted in multiples on a single post.

against the train. This would let the engine perform a 'run-round' manoeuvre or other shunt move, but would be in a strictly defined 'limit of shunt' area. These 'shunt' arms can take several forms, depending on siting and their usage. Some are mounted alongside the main arms on the same post, some are positioned separately, or as they are in low speed areas can be 'ground signals'. These usually take the form of a small rotating disc, which is essentially a compact semaphore arm.

CONTROL

The prototype control of signals can be from one of two sources. The obvious is the signal box, though many branch stations did not possess anything so grand and points and signals were often operated from a ground frame – a small open platform with several levers mounted on or in front of it, and possibly with a small hut built over it to protect the staff member from the weather and contain any other necessary equipment such as a telephone. This frame

The GWR also used 'underslung' arms, as here at Liskeard. Note the bracket-mounted disc below.

Tip

Study photos to see how the real signals either differ or are similar to the kits available. The GWR inherited signals from other companies and you may be able to make something more representative by using the posts or arms from another less obvious kit such as the Ratio LNER or LNWR packs. Don't get locked into the manufacturer's labelling.

was usually locked, but would be released for use by a metal staff that would be carried by the train crew on occupation of the line. Alternatively, the frame was operated by the station team.

One final aspect is the concept of 'one engine in steam'. Essentially this means that the entire branch would be worked as one long single section, thus reducing any signalling to a very basic level. If there is only one engine working, there is nothing to collide with.

There are no hard and fast rules to siting the signals on your layout, save the basic shape given here; every situation will be different. If you are using a prototype track plan, things become somewhat easier as it is possible to obtain the signalling diagram and simply copy it. If you are building a freelance layout, look out for similar track layouts to your model plan and work out what signalling shape is most likely. It is doubtful that you will get it wrong as the prototype was full of variants and anomalies, so you are going to do no worse.

BUILDING A MODEL SIGNAL

There are plenty of model signals available in all the major scales. There are a few ready built, but most come in kit form. This is very sensible as the real thing is so variable, with almost nothing except the lamps being standardized in any way. Ratio once again is the first choice, providing kits in the three main scales, but there are other smaller manufacturers such as Model Signal Engineering, which produces a huge range of brass parts. These

can either be used exclusively, or to customize the Ratio plastic models.

The majority of GWR semaphore signals were of the lower quadrant (L/Q) type, that is, with the arm moving between nine and seven o'clock, with the nine o'clock position indicating stop. Most other companies used (or subsequently moved to) upper quadrant signals (U/Q), which were deemed to be safer, as if any linkage failed the board would fall to a rest position of 'stop'. This was more favourable than a board falling to the 'proceed' position. It is this use of L/Q arms that will immediately tell the viewer that the layout is Great Western. The Ratio kits are designed to represent this, though can be altered either to fit a particular signal as shown further on, or be mixed with other kits in the range to meet other requirements. For example, a model may be of an absorbed line that was fitted with the independent line's signals and then partially refitted with standard GWR equipment; branches could occasionally have an alarming mix of styles.

ADAPTING FOR A PROTOTYPE

The signal chosen for this next project is a starter signal that stood at Towyn (now Tywyn) on the Mid Wales coast. The line was originally built by the Cambrian Railways and is still open today, though the signal in question has long gone. Most of the information was taken from photographs in C.C. Green's books on the line, *The Coast Lines of the Cambrian Railways*. The signal was scaled from the photos and the Ratio kit altered slightly to represent it. This method is applicable to any similar signal and involves close observation of the prototype and the subsequent alteration of certain plastic parts.

PROJECT ELEVEN: STARTER SIGNAL

Materials required:
- Ratio Models GWR signal kit, Ref: 466
- Peco track pins
- Superglue
- Solvent
- Paint.

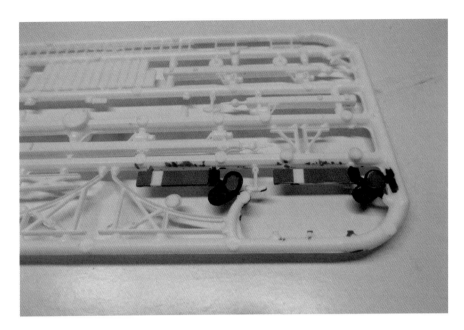

Arms are best given a base coat while still on the sprue.

Tools required:
- File/sanding stick
- Knife
- Small pliers and side cutters
- Tweezers
- Small drills
- Brushes.

EVALUATING THE PARTS

The kit contains three sprues of parts, which, with a bit of cunning, could be used to make up to four signals. Here, a standard height post was used and standard length arm (the GWR generally used 4ft and 5ft (1,200mm and 1,524mm) arms for main signals – these are the latter. A basic single coat of paint was applied while the arms were still on the sprue. Don't worry if it's a little rough at this stage (as here), as it can be tidied up later. Note that the lower glass is actually blue and not green as is often assumed.

The Towyn post was estimated at 16ft high (4,877mm), so the standard post was removed from the sprue and shortened to 64mm. This means that the hole at the foot is lost. This hole was reinstated 12mm up from the bottom using a 0.8mm drill. There

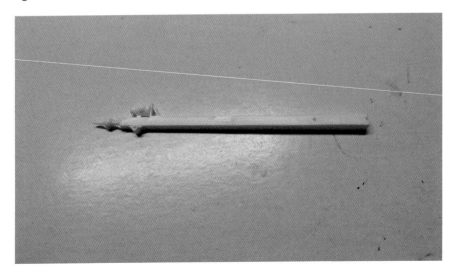

The shortened post.

The arm uses a track pin as a pivot.

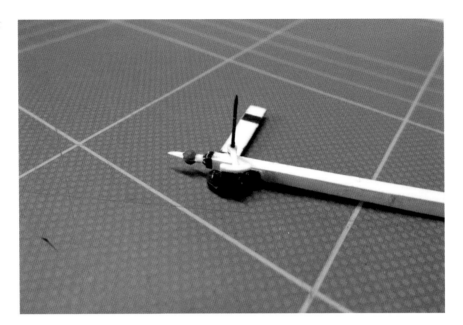

Great care is needed when bending the wire, as the plastic is very fragile.

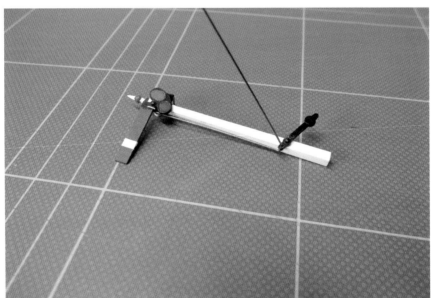

are two sets of lamps/brackets moulded on, but as there was only one arm used, the lower set was removed.

After cleaning up and painting, the hole in the arm was drilled through 0.8mm to clear, and a Peco track pin inserted through it. This was attached with a tiny drop of superglue. The hole in the post was drilled through and, making sure that no glue was present, the pin passed through. The blind, or 'blinker', was fitted in the same way, making sure that the up/down movement corresponded with the arm. Blinds were fitted where the rear of the signal faced the box, meaning that a small light showed when the signal was at danger and was covered when the signal was pulled to 'off', giving the signalman a positive indication of whether the signal was set correctly or not.

The remaining hole in the arm was cleared with a 0.7mm drill and a length of the wire supplied with

A 'stop' can be made from strip or plastic rod.

the kit passed through and bent over. The balance arm was fitted at the foot of the post in the same manner as the semaphore arm and the wire passed through and bent up. Take care during this part as the strength of the wire is far in excess of the plastic and it is easy to break the latter. The wire can be touched up with paint if so required.

At this point, the arms will spin freely without any resistance, so a small 'stop' was fitted to limit the upward movement.

OPERATING SIGNALS

The operation from now on will be down to personal choice. The photos show a basic signal that could be hand-operated by the modeller. For remote operation, the wire could be left at full length, bypassing the balance arm and continuing through the baseboard to a remote control set-up of either a crank and more wire, or a point motor mounted sideways under the board and fitted with suitable stops to limit the travel. The other hole on the balance arm could be used, but this does put quite a bit of strain across what it a very thin piece of soft plastic. In this instance, the use of

extra brass parts would definitely be advantageous by increasing the strength of the linkage.

FITTINGS

Finally, in this instance the ladder was fitted using the black plastic ladder strip included in the kit, which is a little more robust than the white parts also supplied. The photographs of the signal at Towyn show it to have a small rear platform, but unusually no safety loop, so the small platform part from the kit was trimmed slightly and fitted, followed by the ladder, which had been cut to length. Referring to photos in this way firstly demonstrates how signals varied in detail, but also ensures that your model signals represent what actually went on, rather than following some ideal of what people assumed happened. All remaining painting can now be carried out.

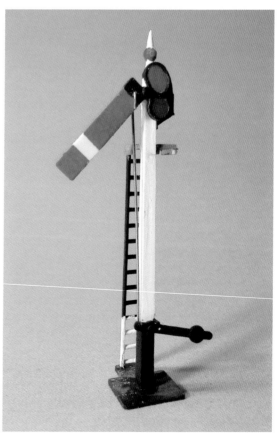

The completed Towyn starter.

Using this method, a number of signals can be built for your layout that are not only prototypical, but unique. Shunt arms could be added to the post if required, as could sighting boards (a white board placed behind the signal arm to improve visibility against dark backgrounds) and telephone boxes and so on. As always, the study of period prototype photographs will give more information and inspiration than any written description.

PROJECT TWELVE: GROUND SIGNAL

Materials required:
• Ratio ground signal kit, Ref: 465
• 2mm plastic tube (optional)
• Superglue
• Solvent
• Paints.

Tools required:
• As per the semaphore signal.

Ratio Models also produces a pack of four ground signals in kit form. These are designed to be built as static items, but could be made to work if you were very keen and nimble-fingered. These are in some ways the most useful item, as the classic terminus would need several of these dotted around the track plan to protect pointwork and siding entry. The kit builds up to a model very similar to that illustrated here, although there were many variants including some with tiny semaphore arms. These, in particular, would make your layout look very different and they are quite easy to make, at least in static form, with just a strip of plastic replacing the disc. Other variants include different post mounting as illustrated. These again could be made using the parts from the kit and simply replacing the supplied post with a length of plastic tubing. Discs were also mounted on main signal posts and one of these is just visible in the photograph of the underslung board shown earlier in this chapter.

Typical ground disc.

Ground discs can also be mounted on posts to aid visibility.

Some ground level discs are mounted on tubular posts.

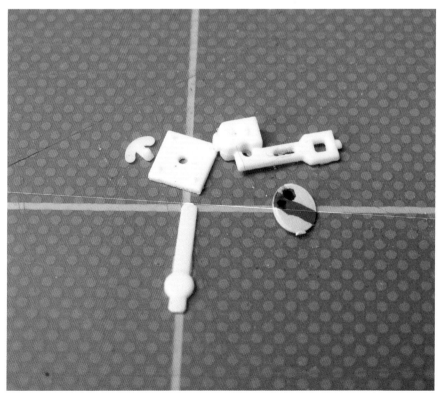

Parts for Ratio ground signal.

Completed ground signal.

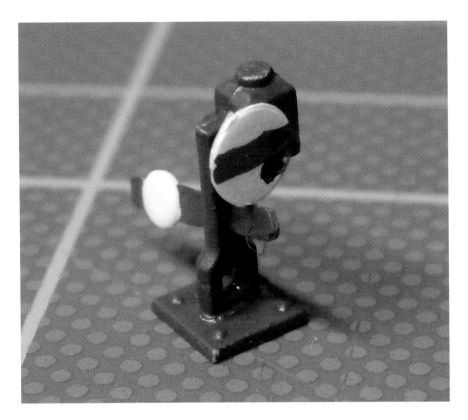

CONSTRUCTING THE GROUND DISC FROM THE RATIO KIT

The kit consists of just four parts and once again a little basic painting while still on the sprue is advantageous. Add the blind first, then the base to the post. Then fit the pre-painted disc and lastly the arm. This construction order is not compulsory, but is far easier. The whole assembly, excepting the front of the disc, can be painted black or Tank Grey. The super-pedantic could add an operating rod to the front of the arm.

Putting these signals on a model layout, even if they are not working, lifts the model considerably, simply because very few people can be bothered to do so. Using the Ratio ground discs and adding a few variations as illustrated will make the scene sparkle even more. Even if you are working in N gauge and wish to replicate this, a disc cut with a leather or button punch and a tiny length of plastic rod should do the trick, finished with a lick of colour. The only problem then would be how to make them operate!

CHAPTER NINE

BRANCH CATTLE TRAFFIC AND AN INTRODUCTION TO ETCHED KITS

CATTLE TRAFFIC

At the beginning of the book it was suggested that 'specials' traffic should be avoided except in extraordinary circumstances. Unless there was a specific point of delivery or pick-up point (such as a dairy), most goods traffic would be carried on the typical branch in simple vans and open wagons. There was one wagon type that does not fall into this category, but was fairly widespread in its use, at least on the rural branches; namely, the humble cattle wagon. Cattle docks were a feature of many country stations, but it should be noted that they did not always command their own sidings, often

being sited on platform bays or loop lines, which clearly illustrates the speed at which the trains had to be loaded and unloaded. The railway company was responsible for carriage of the animals, but not care. Therefore, quick loading was required before any feeding or watering was needed. Most modellers could find use for a small number of cattle wagons on a GWR branch layout and even if a cattle dock is not modelled on the layout, it should be noted that cattle and sheep were sometimes loaded between lines of hurdles (short movable fences) across the passenger platform, or up portable ramps.

The short cattle dock at Highley.

HISTORY

Although livestock had initially been carried on the GWR in open wagons, it was not until the 1850s that specific vehicles were constructed. The early vehicles were built with high sides and without roofs, but by the 1870s something that we would recognize as a cattle wagon was in use all over the GWR. The construction methods generally followed those used for closed vans, beginning with wooden outside-framed bodies and underframes, and developing into steel underframe vehicles with steel body frames and wooden planking. Early period designs used typical short wheelbases of around 8ft (2,438mm) or 9ft (2,743mm), but this was elongated by the end of the nineteenth century to around 11ft (3,353mm) to maximize the loading of what was after all a bulky, but relatively light, load. The GWR cattle wagons were designated a telegraphic code of MEX and were built under the diagram numbers W1 to W12.

The obvious difference between cattle wagons and closed vans was the semi-open sides, The top quarter was usually open except for one or more horizontal bars and there were cut-outs in the lower sides to aid the washing out and the removal of animal waste. The lower sides, ends and underframes mirrored the design of the contemporary vans of the period, although some earlier designs featured low-level cut-outs in the ends as well.

MODELS

Modellers working in the small scales are fairly well catered for: in N gauge there is a lovely late period RTR wagon produced by Peco, which should satisfy most people working in the scale who are modelling a post-1930 period. In OO gauge, there are several kits in plastic, white metal and brass, the most popular being the diagram W1 plastic kit from Cooper Craft. In O gauge, things get a little shakier. There are kits in white metal and brass, but these tend to be from the smaller manufacturers and supply can be sporadic to say the least. Part of the problem could be that as the twentieth-century

chassis designs used the 11ft wheelbase, the manufacturers are unable easily to use the same chassis mould for other model wagons that would typically use 9ft or 10ft (3,048mm) wheelbase lengths. The cattle wagon model may suffer from just being a little different.

PROJECT THIRTEEN: A COOPER CRAFT W5 CATTLE WAGON

Most of the construction techniques used in the building of plastic kits have already been outlined in earlier chapters, so it is unnecessary to repeat them here. However, there are a couple of changes and additions to the kit, so the following will centre around these. The kit represents the W5 vacuum-fitted vehicle, though the W1 is easily built by omitting the vacuum cylinder moulding. Note that the cattle wagons that were vacuum-fitted were designated MEX B.

Materials required:
• Cooper Craft W1/W5 kit, Ref: 1010
• Micro rod in 0.5mm and 1mm diameters
• Wheel sets and bearings
• Solvent
• Paint.

Tools required:
• Knife
• Needle files and sanding stick
• Drills and pin chuck
• Brushes.

BODY MODIFICATIONS

The wagon should be built as per the instructions, but with the following changes. Remove the side mouldings from the sprue and clean up. The horizontal bar is extremely fragile and will almost certainly break. It is not worth trying to repair it; just replace with a length of 0.5mm plastic rod. Mark where the bar enters the central door frame and drill a 0.6mm hole about halfway through. Locate the plastic rod into this hole, add a brush full of solvent and allow to set, checking that it is level and parallel to the side. Trim it to a length just slightly

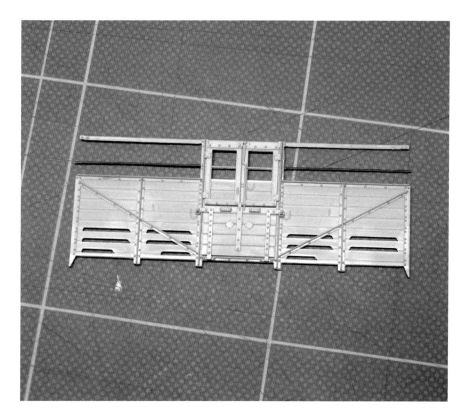

The thin bar can be replaced with microrod.

longer than the side to give yourself some wiggle room for later. Repeat with the other bar on the same side and then again with the other side piece. Put these to one side and turn your attention to the chassis.

CHASSIS

If you are using metal wheels and bearings, fit these first by drilling the axle boxes out to 2mm, then construct the chassis in the usual way. The floor has raised guides for the solebars to rest against, but by setting them out further than this by about 0.5mm helps to get the relationship of the axle/bearing/solebar correct and importantly keeps the solebars vertical. Add the brake parts and run a length of 1mm rod between them. Add the vacuum cylinder and fettle the arm so that it attaches to this rod.

The Dean brake gear is only partially represented in the kit. If you are using scale three link or screw couplings, it would be a simple matter to create a new hanger from strip and run a rod between this and the lever. However, if you are using a standard type of tension-lock coupler, as would be the case here, this becomes impossible, as the coupling will sit in exactly the wrong position for the bar to be fitted.

The rest of the kit can now be constructed as per the instructions, fixing the new horizontal bars to the edges of the ends after trimming to suit.

Tip

Hold a small stock of plastic rod and small-size plastic strip for such repairs and modifications. Don't wait to purchase these until after you have started, as it will speed the construction if you have them to hand. For 4mm scale, two or three sizes of rod, for example 0.5mm, 1mm and 2mm, and strip sizes of 20 × 10thou and 40 × 20thou will cover many minor repairs to wagon strapping and can also be used to fill holes.

The completed Cooper Craft cattle van.

PROJECT FOURTEEN: W12 CATTLE WAGON FROM A DAPOL KIT

Materials required:
- Dapol (or original Airfix) Cattle Wagon
- Plastic rod 1mm
- Plastic strip 40 × 20thou
- Solvent
- Paint.

Tools required:
- As for the previous project.

A LESS OBVIOUS ALTERNATIVE PLASTIC KIT

While the Cooper Craft kit is highly popular, for some reason the kits are now not stocked by so many retailers, so if you want a plastic kit for a cattle wagon, a little sideways thinking is required. The W1/5 wagon is a long-lived early twentieth-century design, but if you are happy running a late-period vehicle, there is an alternative kit which is still of all-plastic construction and is just as freely available. The Dapol (ex-Airfix) British Railways cattle wagon may not be an obvious choice, but the design is rooted with the GWR.

When British Railways was looking for a standard cattle wagon, it first adopted an LMS design, but then widened the brief to include the GWR diagrams. Thus much of the BR fleet was built at Swindon to a shape very close to the last of the GWR vehicles (diagram W12), which were built from 1930. It is therefore a simple enough job to backdate the Airfix/Dapol kit to a W12. This conversion is not 100 per cent accurate – there are a couple of issues, but it will satisfy most modellers, fool most viewers and give variation to a rake of wagons at quite low cost. Either the Dapol or the earlier Airfix kit versions can be used; the Dapol is freely available from the trade, but due to the age of the 1960s mould masters it has more flash on the mouldings. The original Airfix kit is widely available second-hand, is made from a slightly softer plastic, but has cleaner mouldings.

The missing brake parts can be run up from plastic strip and 1mm microrod. The door bangers (arrowed) are best left off until later in the build.

UNDERFRAME

Add the wheel bearings as before and fix the sole-bars to the floor. Add the brakes and then the cross rod as per the previous project. The is no operating arm part included in the kit, so drill a 1mm hole in the vacuum cylinder and add a length of 1mm rod, followed by a section of 40 × 20thou strip. This may need a little fettling to get right, and is slightly impressionistic, but as before adds to the underfloor clutter and makes the underneath appear more realistic. Note that it is best to add the door banger strips to the solebars right at the end of the building process. They are highly vulnerable – here they were added early on and were repaired more than once.

SIDES

One of the main visual differences between the GWR and BR versions is the vertical framing – the GWR's W12 frame stops more or less flush with the bottom of the side, while the BR version drops down to the bottom of the solebar. The close, but not perfect, fix is to cut the lower section off flush, then add a piece of 20 × 10thou strip at the foot to finish the shape of the L-girder frame. Gently remove the over-scale door hinges and file flat. Repeat with the other half of this side, then with both halves of the other side.

The vertical bracing can be visually extended below the floor line by adding short lengths of strip.

DOORS

Drill through the hand hole in the left-hand upper door with a 1.5mm drill and fit to the side using the curved over-scale hinges as a guide. Make sure that it is flat and vertically in line with the side piece. Then when it is set firm, file the hinges flush. Take the lower door, clean up and reduce the size of the 'ears' where the latch would be. Fit under the upper door and fix to the side. You may need to remove a little material with a flat needle file

to get it to sit flush. Then add the second half of the side and the other upper door following the same process. Finally, reduce the thickness and the curve on the lower door hinges. Repeat the whole process with the opposite side, then add one end as shown.

Make up the buffer-beam assembly and remove the dummy three-link coupling sections from the hooks. Then assemble the rest of the wagon except the roof and let all the parts set firmly.

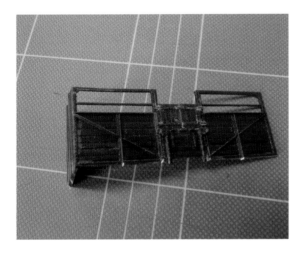

Completed side added to one end.

Adapted buffer-beam assembly. Cast white-metal buffers would further improve.

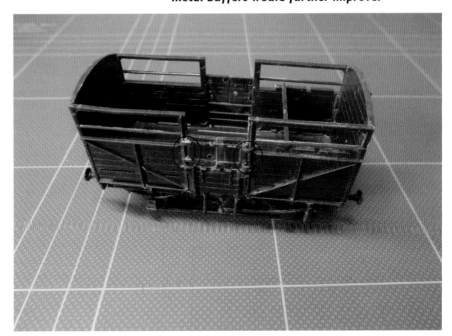

Sides and body together. Highlighted areas show finished and unaltered door hinges.

PAINTING

A couple of base coats can now be applied; Humbrol Tank Grey (67) should be used for the outside. The GWR painted the entire wagon the same colour and this always included the chassis. But before that, give the body a light coat of Dark Earth (29) and the underframe a coat of Leather (62). Let this dry and let it bleed through the grey when that goes over the top. It's a small detail, but it stops the model looking too flat.

The inside should be given a couple of coats of white (mainly to kill the colour of the plastic), followed by a wash of Dark Earth. There is a modellers' myth surrounding cattle wagons that there should be a splashing of white all around the outside lower edges. The truth is, this would only be appropriate for a vehicle operating before the mid-1920s. Lime wash was originally used to disinfect the inside and it spilt through the lower cut-outs, causing the white staining. The practice was discontinued from the 1920s, as the wash was found to damage the hooves of the cattle, so any model set after this time should show much outwardly cleaner wagons. The insides would have been a dirty white or left with bare wood.

FINISHING

The roof can now be added and painted in a pale grey or darker, depending on your assumed running date. Transfers can be from the Pressfix range or Model Master/Fox waterslide sets. Or, as here, a combination of Cooper Craft/Ratio lettering left over from previously built kits can be used. Generally, all kits have spare numbers and these can be rearranged to suit in many cases.

The interior can be given a sloppy coat of dirty white or pale wood colour.

The finished Dapol/Airfix to W12 conversion.

MIX AND MATCH KITS

If you are setting your layout post-1930 as most do and including a short rake of two to three cattle wagons, using these two kits as shown will be adequate, though photographs do show quite long trains on market days. As the development of diagram types between W5 and W12 was a fairly gentle progression, with some careful research and a little ingenuity it would be possible to combine parts from both the Cooper Craft and the Dapol kits to represent some of these types by swapping the ends and altering the doors. (An article by Martin Goodall in *Model Railway Journal* No. 24 details some of these.) The Cooper Craft W1 can even be shortened to represent some of the earlier short wheelbase vehicles built under the W3 diagrams. Which leads neatly on to …

PROJECT FIFTEEN: A SHORT WHEELBASE CATTLE WAGON USING BRASS SIDES

HISTORY

The GWR began a schedule of building general merchandise closed vans entirely from metal in 1886 which continued up to World War I. These wagons were also built for other minor railway companies such as the small Welsh railways, and private operators (see the ex-Spillars version detailed in Chapter Five). Coded as MINK (the designation 'iron mink' is an historian/modeller term – the GWR did not refer to them as such), they were widespread in use, though were superseded by larger wooden designs. The fleet was extensive and included many variants; it numbered over 4,000 vehicles. One of the least successful of these variations was the diagram osL 433 cattle

Iron MINK stands in the sun at Didcot Railway Centre.

wagon. It nominally used iron MINK technology and design, but with semi-open sides and a wooden lower drop-down door.

This cattle wagon variant was built in 1888 and lasted on the Great Western's stock books until 1935. So unsuccessful was the design that only a single vehicle (No. 38010) was constructed. Although the 1935 condemnation date is positive, there is very little known about 380101 and it is more than likely that it was out of service by the 1920s. So why bother to build a model of this failure of a vehicle? There are two reasons: firstly, it is an attractive small cattle wagon that will break up the monotony in a rake of model cattle wagons on your layout. Secondly, there is a conversion kit available that is simple to build and is an easy introduction into handling etched-brass kits. No soldering is necessary as it is possible to use superglue, though you could use solder should you so desire.

Materials required:
• Ratio Iron Mink kit, Ref: 563
• Shire Scenes cattle wagon conversion kit, Ref: S109
• Scrap plastic
• Transfers
• Spray primer
• Superglue (gel)
• Solvent.

Tools required:
• Knife
• Needle files
• Sanding stick
• Small glass-fibre brush.

THE BRASS ETCH

The Shire Scenes conversion kit comprises a single brass etch with seven parts: two sides and five door bolts. The sides should be removed with a large trim-

Tip

When filing against the edge of an etched part, hold it firmly near the work area and file only using a downward motion. Using an up and down sawing motion is likely to end up with the file catching and the part being bent.

FOLDING THE BRASS

Add a thin layer of superglue to the edges of the main part, taking the glue to the part on the tip of a cocktail stick where the new part will attach, and fold the inner side on to the glue. Hold this firmly until the glue cures. Using a gel type glue means that the cure time is slightly slower than standard superglue and timewise gives you a little wiggle room. Drop a blob of glue on to a piece of scrap plastic and transfer it from here to the brass. Do not be tempted to run the glue straight from the tube – this will almost certainly end in tears. There is a glitch on the etch artwork, in that the door hinges are etched the wrong way around. If you have not done so already, remove them and put to one side.

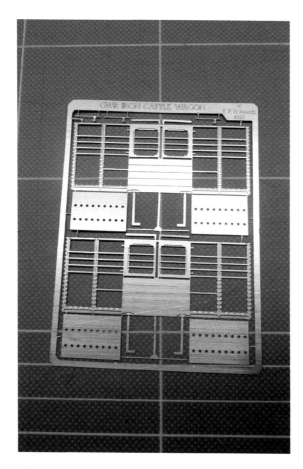

The Shire Scenes fret as supplied.

ming (Stanley) knife over a cutting mat or thick card. There are essentially only two main folds: the larger square lower backing pieces, which fold up behind; and the bracing top and bottom, which fold to the front. Start by removing one side and cleaning any remaining tags with a small file.

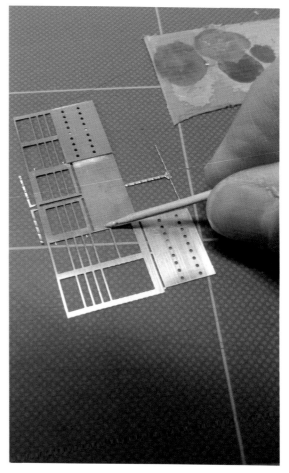

A small amount of superglue can be applied with a wooden cocktail stick.

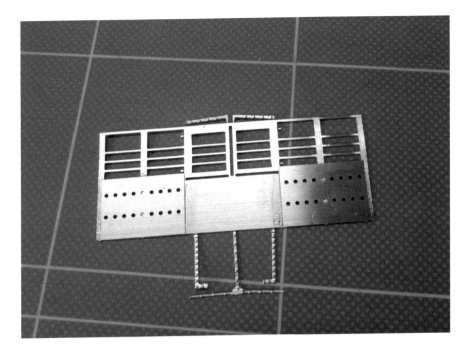

The large side pieces folded up. The strapping goes to the other side, but the outer strapping needs to be swapped left to right.

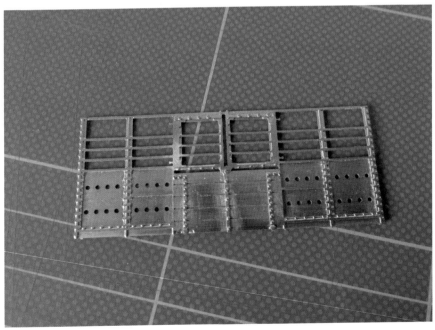

Finished side. Note the reversed strapping in the correct position.

Using the same glue application technique, fold the 'T'-shaped bracing up from the bottom and attach; similarly, the bracing part can be folded down from the top. Then add the now loose hinges, reversing their original orientation so that they now turn outward. Finally, add the tiny coach bolts as shown in the instructions; there is a spare included on the etch just in case you should lose one. The side is now complete. Carefully clean any surplus glue away with a glass-fibre brush and repeat the process with the second side.

CHASSIS

The sides are designed to replace the sides on a Ratio Models iron MINK kit. This is an old kit in the range and has an unusual design, in that the solebars and the sides are moulded in one single piece, so the first job is to tackle the removal of the sides. Leave the part on the sprue, as this gives more for you to hold on to. Using a brand-new blade, make several light knife cuts along the join as shown. The side is effectively a waste item, so work on this side of the join rather than the solebar side. Remove the chassis part from the sprue, clean the part up and repeat the process for the other side.

Add bearings to the solebars in the manner described for earlier plastic kits, add the solebars to the chassis and add the single brake shoe assembly. The remaining V hanger on the opposite side can be removed at this stage. A second set of brakes was allegedly added to the vehicle late in its life, so if you wished to do this a second set of brake moulds would need to be sourced separately.

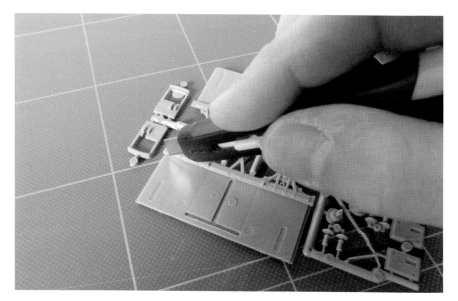

The solebars should be cut off as shown, though they should be held firmly (or clamped to the bench) to steady.

Solebars and brakes added to the floor. The dust indicated that there is a little tidying to do with a file or sanding stick.

THE ENDS

The ends are briefly mentioned in the instructions, but no detail is given. This can be one of the problems in dealing with a very minor historical item. Enough real details to build a model are often sparse and assumptions need to be made, or have previously been made. The Ratio MINK ends represent those of a ventilated general merchandise van and therefore include wedge-shaped ventilator covers that would have let fresh air in but kept the rain out, though it seems unlikely that a cattle wagon with 30 per cent open sides would have needed extra ventilation. Coupled with that, the only prototype photograph available is the works portrait, which is taken square-on and the ends are annoyingly not visible. This leaves a hanging question: Do you build the cattle wagon with the ends as provided, or adjust your thinking to the 'no vent' logic?

Here, the latter course was taken and the vents were removed by very gently filing with a flat needle file, taking care not to damage the rivet detail on the end bracing. The plastic does become paper thin at the foot of the vent, but it is just about achievable. The ends can now be attached to the chassis as per the Ratio instructions using a square edge to ensure that they are vertical.

The end vents can be carefully filed off, leaving a paper-thin section.

The ends can be added, but must to be completely vertical.

The main alteration to the Ratio plastic parts finished.

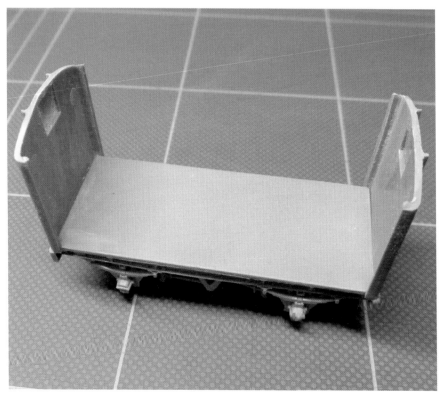

FITTING THE SIDES

The completed brass sides can now be fitted to the ends. There may be a little discrepancy in the gap between the ends. The sides have a natural lip generated by the inner side pieces. This lip should overlap the ends slightly. If it doesn't, a little remedial work on the ends with a needle file is needed to reduce them very slightly to allow a good fit.

The new brass sides are roughly half the thickness of the original plastic parts and a small gap is present between them and the edge of the floor, so some secondary packing is needed. You could add a strip of plastic along the length of the floor on both sides to bring the width out to match, or as here just add a little packing from scrap plastic. Some sort of bracing bar will certainly be required along the top edge. Once again, scrap plastic can be used and stuck with superglue. Both of these additions will stop the sides bowing inward when the wagon is undoubtedly handled in the normal manner by gripping with the thumb and finger over the doors.

Any further parts such as buffers and brake details should now be added. The wagon can now be cleaned up and given a light coat of primer from a spray can (auto paint is more than adequate). This draws all the different materials together and will bring any mistakes to the fore. The inside can be painted as per the earlier plastic kit models and the roof can be added.

The brass sides added along with plastic scrap reinforcement to stop them bowing inward.

A light coat of auto primer draws all the parts together. The roof is a loose fit at this point.

The finished and weathered iron van. Lettering is a mix of Cooper Craft and Ratio left over from previous projects.

FINISHING

Once again, there is a general lack of historical detail available, so a certain amount of assumption comes into play. The works photo and the instructions illustration show the wagon in the original 1880s painting style. This will probably not be appropriate for most modellers, who will be working in a later period. Therein lies a problem, as a little guesswork regarding what might have happened is involved.

We can probably safely assume that the wagon was repainted at least once during its life, so one of the larger twentieth-century lettering schemes would have been applied. The physical problem is that there is not any clear space in the usual positions at either side of the door, so in this case the larger lettering has been added to the door in a similar style to the passenger-rated 'brown' vehicles.

CHAPTER TEN

SMALL BUILDINGS AND ANCILLARY EQUIPMENT

Aside from the large main structures at a branch-line station, the modeller will usually wish to add those small, but highly important, buildings and items that allow the railway to function efficiently. As far as the GWR is concerned, these are mostly no different to any other British railway company, but one or two are quite iconic and very much help to set the scene – that all-important 'recognize the place before the train turns up' aspect which is critical in getting the feel right on a model layout. So although these next few items are small in model terms and quite quick to construct, they are definitely worth a more detailed look.

GWR CAST PLATFORM SEATS

Most early seating on the GWR was of the basic rustic four wooden-leg variety. These were susceptible to water ingress and were gradually replaced by a pure GWR design comprising cast feet/backs and timber cross pieces. These were further identifiable as being a GWR item by the use of the company's scroll design set into the feet.

From 1934, the roundel insignia (or 'shirt button') design was introduced throughout the locomotive and rolling-stock fleets and this was also matched by a new design of seat, now with a solid foot containing the roundel in a solid raised casting. Considering that these were only produced from 1934–46, they have been incredibly long lived and not only are they still to be seen on the modern system today, but they are also scattered throughout the preserved railways and even available in replica form to the general public through one or two garden furniture companies. Local painting styles for these seats varied, but the safe decision for the modeller would be the light stone/mid-stone combination.

Original GWR scroll styling seat.

Later seat styling.

It was originally thought that the cast seats may not have worked their way out to the more rural branches, but a brief study of Paul Karau's *Great Western Branch Line Termini* confirms that they did and out of the ten stations detailed in this book only Tetbury and Hemyock do not appear to have been supplied. A word of caution though – yes, they are there, but if you wish to be accurate, there is usually only one per platform, in a couple of cases two, but never more than this. Scattering a long line of seats along your model branch-line platform would be overdoing it somewhat. As in most things, a lightness of touch is always preferable.

PROJECT SIXTEEN: GWR SEATS

Materials required:
• Cooper Craft GWR Platform Seats
• Solvent

• Paint.

Tools required:
• Knife
• Sanding stick/file
• Brushes.

GWR SEATS IN MODEL FORM

Models of the GWR seats have long been available from Cooper Craft in both designs, but alternatives are the laser-cut versions from Metcalfe Models and Roxey Moulding in 4mm scale, Severn Models in 2, 4 and 7mm scales and CPL Models in 7mm. Here, the Cooper Craft kit has been used to make up one of the original designs. You have to choose which design to build as there is only one set of planking, but it would not be beyond the capability of most modellers to make a further set from some 20thou plastic sheet, thus doubling the number of seats able to be produced should you require them.

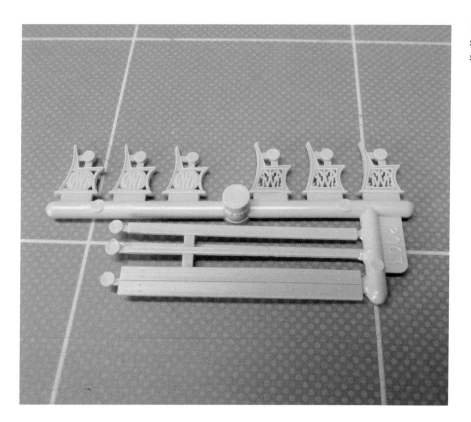

The Cooper Craft seat kit parts as supplied.

The uprights are best fitted upside down on a block of wood or a similar non-plastic surface.

Completed GWR seat.

Working on a non-plastic block, such as a piece of scrap timber, add the cast feet to the lower seat. Then, when these have hardened off, add the two planks for the back and paint.

GWR PAGODA BUILDINGS

When thinking about recognizable items other than rolling stock that are instantly linked to the GWR, the pagoda hut comes pretty high on the list. These are in essence a strange design for a railway, in that a building supplying a basic requirement has one of the most overblown design attributes. Nevertheless, they were more than most things a standard GWR item – 'Standard Type A shelter'. There were many variants and alterations over the years, but they were used as passenger shelters, lock-up platform stores and lamp huts throughout the system. There were even a number of copycat pagoda huts used on the Southern Railway.

Obviously for the modeller the tricky bit is going to be the roof, but help is at hand. Bachmann offers a

ready to plant resin model in 4mm scale and Farrish the same in 2mm scale. If kit building in the smaller scale is to your taste, then P.D. Marsh produces a white-metal kit in 2mm as well. Wills produces a pagoda as part of its Scenic Series in 4mm scale, which is well made and captures the pagoda's shape, 'capture' being the operative word here. With a slice of classic model manufacturer's compression, the kit comes out at a scale 5ft (1,524mm) too short and a shade too wide to boot. Does this make it a bad choice for your layout? Well, that is up to the modeller. Most will be happy to use it as it is and it would be a very straight-forward 'cut and shut' conversion to combine two kits to gain the extra length. As the kit is only around £5 to buy, this is still a reasonable amount to spend and the leftover bits can be used elsewhere, making it all quite efficient.

The pagodas were generally built locally to a specified GWR drawing to two basic types – with windows and without. The windows were metal framed units, possibly shipped in direct from Swindon. The building itself was 3ft (915mm) wide corrugated

Pagoda shelter with front and end windows, plus locally added doors.

Internal detail of the Didcot shelter.

sheeting over a timber frame. The lock-up versions were usually plain, the passenger shelters built with windows and fitted with internal seating. A few were subsequently altered to include end windows and there was at least one double-length version and a triple if period photos are to be believed.

The next project is a quick essay in kit alteration and could be used as a warm-up before tackling the larger station buildings in Chapter Seven.

PROJECT SEVENTEEN: END-WINDOW PAGODA SHELTER

This project takes the route of using the basic Wills kit and altering it to produce an end-window version. This is highly compromised on several levels as explained earlier, as it is unaltered with regard to length, but it will give the modeller a little practice in a couple of techniques and also produce a model that is different to all the thousands of unmodified Wills pagodas on model railway layouts.

Materials required:
• Wills kits, Refs: SS 35 and SS 86
• Plastic strip 20 × 40thou
• Plastic sheet 30thou and 20thou
• Liquid solvent
• Paint.

Tools required:
• Craft knife or scalpel
• Sanding stick
• Needle file (flat)
• 1.5mm drill and pin chuck
• Pencil
• Brushes.

The photo shows what you get in the kit, plus a Peco window that was originally considered before construction commenced. It was finally decided that the smaller Wills window would be better suited and that is the first job to carry out. The moulding is

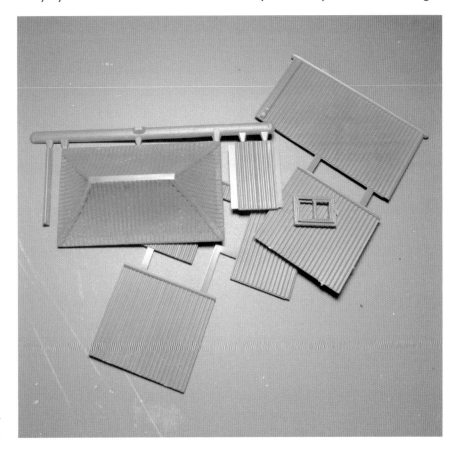

The parts for construction.

The bars on the Wills window units can be thinned down with a needle file.

good, but in this case the vertical bars were carefully thinned using a flat needle file to represent the likely metal framed units usually used.

FITTING THE WINDOWS

Take one end and smooth off the circular 'witness' mark from the rear face. (*Witness marks are the usually circular [raised or depressed] marks on the rear of injection moulded plastic parts.*) Mark the centre line (17mm) and draw a line 12mm up from the foot, followed by a second 13mm up from the first. Then using the centre line mark 6mm either side and finish the box, which should be 12mm wide by 13mm high.

Then 'chain drill' *inside* the lines marked as shown with a 1mm or 1.5mm drill. Cut between these holes with a knife (working away from each corner) to release the middle, then carefully file back to the line with a combination of sanding stick and flat needle file. Fit the window behind and fix with solvent. Then add a simple windowsill from 20 × 40thou plastic strip. Repeat the process with the other end.

The end window openings are marked out on the rear.

The chain drill method is used here to remove the plastic.

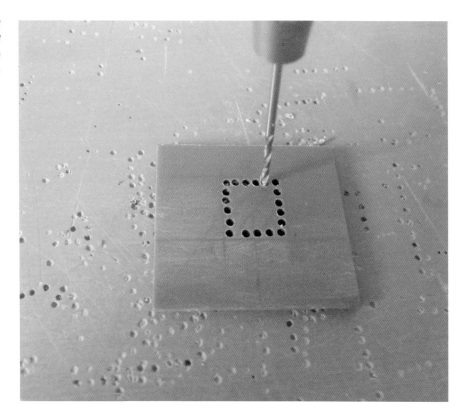

The Wills window fitted into the end wall.

A rudimentary seat can be added from scrap plastic sheet.

Clean up the wall parts and assemble the rear and ends. Cut a strip of 30thou plastic sheet 4mm wide and to a length to fit the inside. Mount this 6mm from the ground level and add a couple of supports from a 3mm length of the same material. The pedantic may wish to add internal framing as illustrated in the photos, which would be lovely but it will be tricky to see it once the hut is on the layout.

MAKING THE DOORS

The doors are influenced by those on a pagoda on the preserved Llangollen Railway in North Wales and are a simple vertical board design with timber framing (though interestingly these play against accepted building practices and appear to be hung the wrong way up). As the doors will be fixed open it is this framing which takes centre stage. Using 20thou sheet mark up both doors as shown end to end, each 25 × 8mm. Then mark up 2mm planks and scribe using the tip of the knife held at right angles to the work. Do this before the doors are cut from the sheet, as it gives you something to handle rather than fiddling with small pieces of plastic.

Cut a 2mm wide strip of the same 20thou sheet, about 110mm long. Make pencil marks 2mm from

Doors are marked out in pencil and scribed with a craft knife held at 90 degrees to the line.

The framing is built up with more sheet and solvent.

each end of each door and another at each centre point. Work down the doors, sticking the strip across with solvent and cutting off when set, then moving to the next. Then add the diagonals in the same way. The photo should make this clear. Note that there is a right and a wrong way to position these – the pencil marks show how. Finally, carefully cut the doors from the sheet.

PAINTING

Before the doors are added, paint the entire wall assembly and the separate roof. As the plastic is dark, it will certainly need two to three coats. As with most lineside buildings the painting colours varied wildly from pure GWR standard paint colours through to entirely black via whites and rust along the way. Put 'GWR pagoda shelters' into an Internet search engine and you will get plenty of examples of these paint variations. Here the plan, unlike most projects in this book, was to go with a reasonably unweathered condition and copy the museum quality of the Didcot Railway Centre shelter pictured.

Lastly finials can be added to the roof using short lengths of 20 × 40thou strip that have been sanded to a point. Give the shelter any final paint coats,

Finials can be added to the roof using plastic strip.

Doors added.

The completed modified Wills pagoda shelter.

paint the window frame white and add glazing (20 × 20mm) behind using the bubble packaging from the kit. Add the doors and roof and you're done.

GWR LAMP HUTS

The humble lamp hut is one of those insignificant railway items that is not often given a second glance by most people, is probably way down the list in the planning of a model railway, and yet in reality is one of the most important railway buildings. The steam railway ran by lamp; pure and simple. The signals had lamps to shine through the spectacle glasses, all trains carried between one and three at the rear and the locomotive carried a set of lamps at the front. It's easy after having several generations of car drivers to forget that front illumination and signalling was not standard on a steam locomotive. Front illumination was almost zero (even with the lamps), but what was important was the locomotive being visible to the signalman and other rail workers, not only to see that it was approaching, but to be able to tell quickly what sort of train was behind it. Lamps were arranged in set formations at the front to show if the train was

Typical GWR lamp hut with a single door in the end and no roof vent.

an express passenger, stopping train, goods and so on. All of these lamps needed storing and maintaining when not in use in a place that was not only secure from thieves, but, as they were fuelled by oil, as fire-proof as possible. Therefore, the entire rail system was covered in small tin sheds with minimal window arrangements to store lamps, fuel and related equipment. Simple and dull to the casual viewer, but highly necessary to the working of the railway.

LAMP HUT MODEL KITS

The simplest way of adding a lamp hut is to use one of the several kits that are available. In 4mm scale, the Wills double pack will get you started quickly and cheaply, though there is (as usual) a query or two on the design. The first is the mounting bracket on one of the sides for fire buckets. As you can see from the prototype photographs, this is not a common addition. The second similar issue is the circular vent on the roof moulding. There is one such vent on the lamp hut that stood at the back on the platform at the GWR's Ashburton station, so there is some reference for it, but again it's not a common fitting.

Getting rid of these is fairly straight-forward and of course there are other modifications you can make for what were a range of varied designs.

PROJECT EIGHTEEN: WILLS LAMP HUT

Materials required:
• Wills Lamp hut kit, Ref: SS22
• Plastic strip 10 × 20thou and 20 × 40thou
• Solvent
• Paint.

Tools required:
• Needle files
• Sanding stick
• Knife
• Brushes.

REFINING THE PARTS

The parts for the main structure consist of four walls and a roof (there are two huts in the pack). The possible non-requirement of the bucket fitting can be approached in two ways. The first is simple: turn the

The extraneous mouldings can be removed with a rat-tail needle file.

The roof vent can be removed in a similar fashion.

hut around so that the offending wall does not face the viewer, or swap the sides around to get the same result. If this is not possible, the second option is carefully to remove the offending moulding.

Firstly, pare away as much plastic as possible with a very sharp craft knife, working downward and keeping your fingers well out of the way. Then remove more plastic with the sanding stick, taking the extraneous mould down to point level with the top of the corrugations. Finally, using an oval (rat-tail) needle file, file each corrugation 'dip' and remove the last traces of the moulding.

The base for the vent on the roof moulding can be treated in the same fashion, excepting the first action with the knife, which should be unnecessary.

ADDING DETAILS

The window at the rear is quite an odd shape. Most of the windows on lamp huts are portrait style, but this is landscape and only has a pair of window bars. In order to change it from all the other Wills lamp huts, add a couple of short pieces of 10 × 20thou plastic strip as shown to increase the window from a

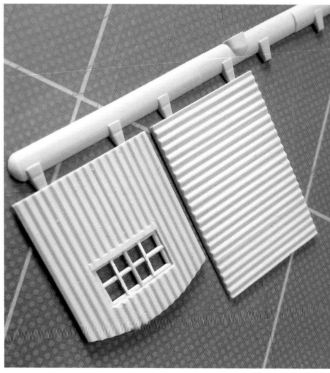

Extra window bars can be added to suit with plastic strip.

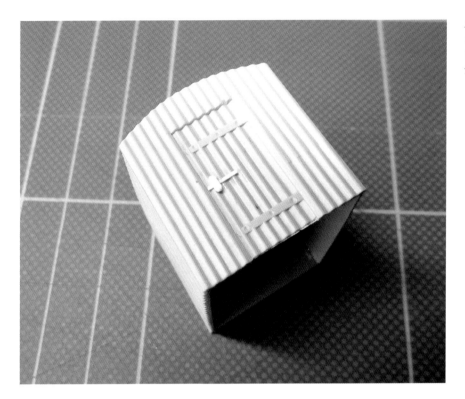

A hasp and padlock can be suggested using small pieces of plastic.

four-pane to an eight-pane model. Although this does not alter the shape, it does turn it slightly toward something for which security is important.

Some doors were mounted from the outside, some from the inside. The kit represents the latter type, but a tiny extra detail can be added in the form of a hasp and padlock. The hasp is simply a length of 10 × 20thou again, the padlock can be formed by rounding a piece of 20 × 40thou strip, sticking it to the hasp and trimming to shape when the joint is fully cured. This can be added to the door at the appropriate place.

FINISHING AND PAINTING

The roof can now be fitted and glazing added to the rear wall. It should be noted that the kit's roof is not too generous in length. There is not much you can do about this, but one possible fix is to take a millimetre or so off the length of the side pieces, resulting in just a little overhang.

The finished colours of lamp huts ranged from the standard GWR colour schemes to all-over black. The huts were fairly low in the painting schedule

and a coat of bitumen paint would often be used to restrain the onset of rust. The roofs seem to be a particular problem, or perhaps they just did not get the attention that the walls did. Here the kit was finished as per the preserved example at the Didcot Railway Centre, but with a light touch of weathering in the form of some dry-brushing and washes.

WATER TOWERS

All steam railways need water and lots of it. So there are very few situations where some sort of model water supply would not be required on a layout. Water cranes can be provided on platforms – though these are great thieves of visual platform length, which will probably already be at a premium on the layout, so unless you are working strictly to a proto-type, it is worth siting the water supply somewhere else. The alternative to the platform crane type is the water tower. These can be square or round, on legs or on brick or stone bases, but the iconic GWR tower is the round tank on a single pillar. These were built in various sizes with either a coned or a flat top,

Hut at Bodmin Parkway with offset door and bitumen coating.

Completed and weathered Wills lamp hut.

although it should be noted that these pillar type towers were not exclusive to the GWR and were by no means the only design of water tower used by the company.

A MODEL TOWER

The modeller is well supplied in 4mm scale with kits from Peco and Ratio, with items from Peco in N and Skytrex in O gauge. The next project takes the excellent 4mm scale Ratio kit and adapts it to something closer to the small round water tower that stood at Hemyock up until the 1960s.

Large pillar tank with conical top.

Tank with flat top.

PROJECT NINETEEN: SMALL FLAT-TOP WATER TOWER

Materials required:
- Ratio GWR pillar water tower, Ref: 528
- Fine chain
- Superglue
- Paint.

Tools required:
- Razor saw
- Carpenter's square (optional)
- Files
- Drills and pin chuck
- Sanding stick
- Brushes.

CUTTING THE TANK

The kit is accompanied by an exploded diagram type instruction sheet with a numbered order. It would be possible to follow this, but here it was decided to build up parallel sub-assemblies. The post and base should be tackled first, making sure that the post is exactly vertical. The tank can be tackled next. There are lines moulded inside to help you reduce the size of the tank, but as an almost 50 per cent reduction is needed for the Hemyock tower this would require two cuts, thus increasing the likelihood of error. Using the panel join line around the outside it is possible to reduce the tank height by around half with only one cut. The best way is to cut just outside the line with a razor saw and file back to the line rather than trust accurate sawing. When this has been tidied up, join the two halves and add the top and bottom pieces.

Fix the completed tank to the post, making sure that it is completely level and parallel. Using a high fixed square edge, such as a book or carpenter's square, put the tank in place and rotate the whole assembly against this square edge until you are completely satisfied that all is well. Even a few degrees out will show on the finished model and will jump out at you every time you look at it. It's easier in the long run to take a little time and get it right at this juncture.

Basic assembly with pillar and cut-down tank.

PIPEWORK

Drill a 0.6mm hole through the pipe where indicated on the instruction sheet and also drill a further hole at the very front a few millimetres above the last joint. Add a short section of wire into this hole using superglue. Then add the pipe to the bottom of the tank, again making sure that it is absolutely level. Then add the support wires and attach into the pre-drilled holes.

Finally, add the 'step' support to the post. Putting the support on beforehand will give you less room for manoeuvre if the pipe moulding is a little too short after finishing. Working downward from the tank is easier than trying to get an accurate tank/pipe/step sandwich.

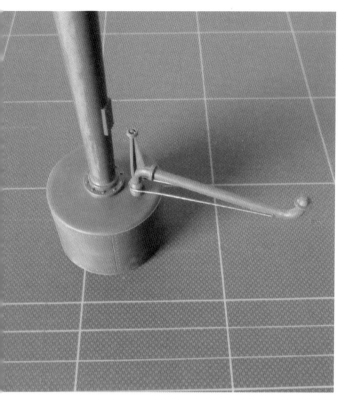

Exit pipe added with wire supports fitted.

Tip

Fine chain has a multitude of uses on a layout and can be purchased through tool dealers such as Squires or Eileen's Emporium, but it is also worth keeping an eye out for scrap jewellery chain, which is available in charity shops and at the lower end of the antiques dealers' trade for mere pence.

TOP FITTINGS

The brass fittings for the top of the tank can now be added. You may wish to give the whole assembly a rough coat of paint first, as a pale colour such as the GWR's stone over the battleship grey plastic is an uphill climb and it needs a bit of a head start.

A long length of chain can be added to the operating arm using a loop of fine scrap wire (a strand of layout wire is ideal). This chain can be hooked over the spigot of wire that was added to the front of the pipe and fixed with a drop of superglue.

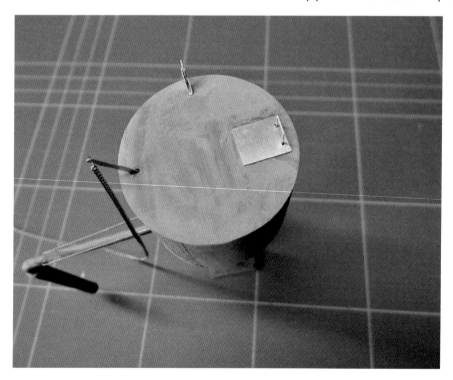

Tank top details added with first coat of paint.

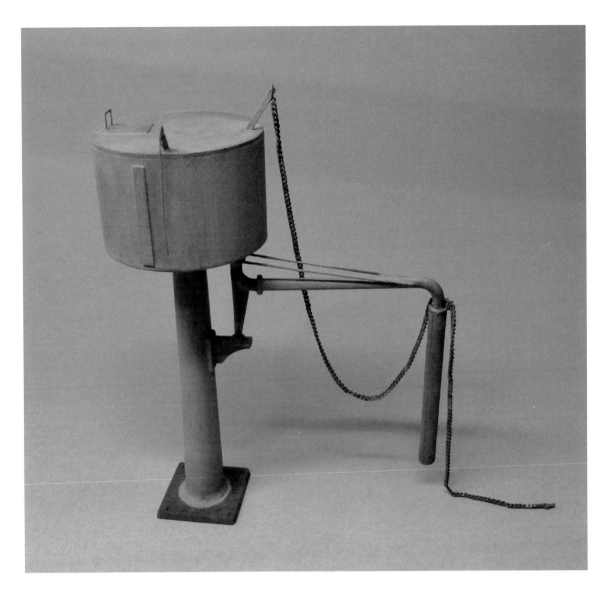

Tank completed. The right-hand chain will be attached to a short retaining post when fitted on the layout.

FINISHING OFF

The water bag can now be added to the end of the pipe. This is made from a slippery engineering plastic and will need a little bit of fettling to fit and will require superglue to attach to the pipe. A second length of chain can be added to the wire spigot and

glued. In reality, this would be hooked over a timber post set a few feet away, which would stop the pipe swinging in the wind. This post can be added (along with the tank's access ladder) when the tank is finally fitted on to the layout.

CHAPTER ELEVEN

PLANNING YOUR LAYOUT

PLANNING

So, you have decided on the Great Western branch line as a prototype subject. Let's also assume you have decided to model in the popular 4mm scale (OO) and that you have a few pieces of 4mm scale equipment to hand. These may or may not be suitable, but even if they don't fit the overall brief, they can be used in the planning stages as props and to check clearances. Where, then, is the best place to start? Well, you ideally need to make a few paper sketch plans and ideas. These could include several different aspects – domestic space, cash considerations, and so on. However, there are a couple of overriding questions: What do you want your layout to be of and what do you want to achieve with it? Here are a few possibilities:

- a multi-station branch around a large room
- an L-shaped branch through-station along two walls of a room
- a small exhibition layout
- a country terminus
- a goods-only branch.

Any of the above are feasible. The first will take a little longer. The last three suggest something that could be finished in a reasonable timescale, with the goods-only branch being the most economical as no passenger stock needs to be purchased or built. It would be possible to exhibit any of the suggestions to some degree, but this needs careful thought and other non-modelling factors have to be allowed for, such as transport, weight, portability and public operation issues. This last point is introduced early as it can have quite a profound effect on how a layout is designed and built, so it needs to be considered right from the start. A home layout will probably not require extra lighting/display boards/portable power units and to be operated from the rear, but an exhibition layout most probably will, therefore these should be factored into the planning/design/thought process right from the start. This issue is covered in more depth in the next chapter.

There is always the question of whether to build a terminus or a through-station. Both have their downsides, but a terminus is often the best choice for a small exhibition layout, as a through-station by its very nature will need a storage yard at each end for the trains to 'disappear' to and this extra floor space taken up with no scenic model on it often creates more problems than it solves.

BEING REALISTIC

Many years ago, not only was railway modelling a rich man's pursuit, but it was also a main-line affair. As the hobby got cheaper and the scales got smaller, the view was put about that the way into the hobby was to start with a branch-line terminus and work this into a main-line layout as funds allowed. The upshot of this idea was that branch lines became not only the start point, but, contrary to the original idea, the finish as well, though the primary idea is a sound one. Even if you have dreams of a room-filling layout, starting with a smaller GWR branch terminus does two things: a) it lets you learn the modelling techniques before spending too much on the large infrastructure; and b) it enables you to build your stud of rolling stock gradually without it looking stupidly lonely on a large layout. A small branch terminus is going to ease you in gently and can always be broken up for parts or sold on as a more ambitious layout emerges.

Maurice Hopper's scratch-built wagons in S scale.

Alternatively, if you chose the first idea of a multi-station branch in a large room, building one section at a time before moving on to the next allows you to work your skills and the rolling stock up without committing too much. A room full of huge areas of bare baseboards is also guaranteed to drag a project into the category of 'millstone'. Building and finishing one smaller section, possibly exhibiting it, and then, and only then, moving on to the next is a fine way of progressing.

BASING YOUR MODEL ON THE PROTOTYPE

Another mantra that is often bandied about is: 'base your model on the prototype and not on other people's models'. In most cases this is sound advice and the small GWR branch-line terminus is a useful tool. Ashburton in Devon is often cited as a perfect terminus plan, especially for the novice, though there are glitches in the operation, as some of the shunting on the prototype was carried out using a chain, which is not easy to replicate in the smaller scales. In

this situation, the modeller has to use a little artistic licence, commonly known as 'freelancing'. This is not a dirty word; many modellers who preach about the perfection of prototype modelling rarely produce anything that has not been compressed in some way, or has the correct rolling stock augmented with 'other items'. For instance, pretty branch termini such as Ashburton or St Ives were run with only limited types of locomotive power through much of their lives, but this does not mean that you can't model something based on them and vary the motive power. A logical way to approach this, especially for the beginner, is to take elements of two or three sites and combine them to create something which gives the best and widest range of options.

Taking that other chestnut of advice: 'you should be able to identify the place/area without any trains in view', what we should do on a model is to establish the type of combination to create a typical scene that tells the viewer where the layout is set. In doing this, the appearance of a GWR train is enhanced ten-fold as it looks right and the overall scene is complete. That does not mean that you have to stuff every

Andy Cundick's Cambrian layout. The buildings immediately set the place and railway company.

Great Western modelling item described in this book on to your layout; in fact, this is best avoided. Decide where you want the layout set and which items will best set the scene in the most natural way and will tell the viewer that this scene is typical of the prototype, even if the whole thing is basically freelance. Here are a few examples:

• standard GWR paint schemes on signs and wood-work
• conical water tower

Tip

Look at the general area in which you wish to set your model and take note of factors such as geology, building materials/styles and other local details. Even if you live outside of the GWR area, photo books and Internet study such as using Google Earth can give you all you need without leaving your house.

- broad-gauge building doorways and track spacing
- constituent company signal boxes
- lower quadrant signals.

APPLYING THE SENSE OF PLACE TO ROLLING STOCK

The late Bob Barlow, ex-editor of *Model Railway Journal*, was often quoted as saying 'It is the art of the typical which convinces.' This gem of sage thought should be pinned on the wall of every modelling room. What Bob Barlow meant was that in order to make a scene on a layout believable it should demonstrate and reflect the most likely of backgrounds and rolling stock, and avoid the unusual, special or quirky elements. We all love to run favourite stock – and that is all well and good, but if we, in this case, want to model the Great Western Railway at a particular period of time, the models we buy or build should reflect what the GWR typically looked like and not how we imagine it looked. This point has been mentioned several times already, but is remarkably important – the non-acceptance of what the model manufacturers push at us and instead looking closely at what really happened and trying to capture the particular look and feel of it.

'Try' is used deliberately. We do not as a rule have large swathes of domestic space, unlimited funds or the time to replicate everything exactly. This is particularly so when it comes to linear ground measurements, as even a small branch terminus can easily stretch out to 9m (30ft) long in 4mm scale if you work exactly to scale. What we can do is 'try' to gain the feel of what went on with the background as detailed above and particularly by using typical rolling stock. Before you buy an RTR model or a kit, ask yourself why you are doing this and attempt a little research as to the viability of such a model. That is not saying that everything should be prescriptive, only that if an image of reality is your goal, then starting by looking at the reality first, and not guessing what it might be, will give you a greater chance of achieving that, along with the praise and adulation from possible future observers.

HISTORICAL STUDY

There is a problem in that the more you find out, the harder things get, and as you study the histories of specific GWR locomotives and stock, where they ran and what sort of trains they might have hauled, the fussier you will become. If you want to get the 'feel' right, this 'art of the typical' should be the question you ask over and over again. If this becomes your mantra, the result will be far more satisfying and realistic than if you just follow the crowd and design your layout out of the RTR manufacturers' catalogues. Note that 'accurate' was not used; there is a difference. If being totally accurate is your aim, then all well and good. A far more achievable goal is 'typical' or 'likely'. Find that typical and overwhelmingly Great Western feel, and the magic will appear. Make accurate your goal and you may get it perfect, but miss the atmosphere by a mile.

THE BRANCH TERMINUS AS A PLAN

The theory of this is easy enough to deal with, and of course the same arguments could be levelled at any railway model in any scale from anywhere in the world. It has to be said that some layouts have 'it', and some don't, and a lot of the time it is being 'typical', rather than overly accurate, that tips the balance. How, then, do you set about it in real terms? The best way is to choose your subject and gather as much visual information as possible. It does not have to be all concerning the same line; it could be a combination of lines as outlined above. Then sketch out a plan. This could take the form of track diagrams and signal positions, but also a list of items that may be applicable. It could be a rough list with accompanying sketches on a sheet of A4 file paper.

As you can see from the illustration, this is certainly no hi-tech exercise, but is essential for a layout to work. It need not take more than five or ten minutes to do and there should ideally be several of these before you get anywhere near drawing or measuring out the plan full size. What it does do is empty all the ideas out on to paper where they can be seen

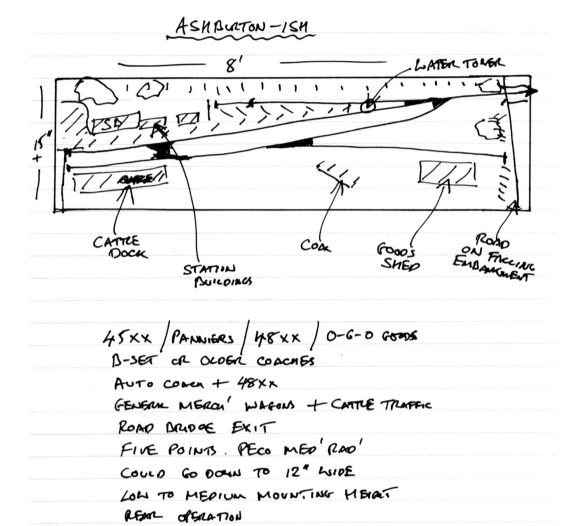

ASHBURTON-ISH

45xx / PANNIERS / 48xx / 0-6-0 GOODS
B-SET or OLDER COACHES
AUTO COACH + 48XX
GENERAL MERCH' WAGONS + CATTLE TRAFFIC
ROAD BRIDGE EXIT
FIVE POINTS. PECO MED'RAD'
COULD GO DOWN TO 12" WIDE
LOW TO MEDIUM MOUNTING HEIGHT
REAR OPERATION

Initial sketch of small layout idea inspired by Ashburton with ideas of stock and other design factors.

and edited in a much easier way than in your mind's eye. This is by no means the finished product and the potential layout will go through many changes and substitutions before building commences.

Also note that the locomotive roster is not only small, but dedicated to the layout type. The biggest locomotive is the Dean Goods – this could be a Collett Goods or a Dukedog class instead – but this is the maximum in terms of size. If you want to run large locomotives that look at home, sketch out a layout that visually fits (an MPD would be a better

plan for this in a similar space). Note also that there are rough board measurements: 8ft ×15in (2,440 × 381mm). These are what would possibly work, but it may be necessary to stretch the length to accommodate the plan. Conversely, it may be possible to compress slightly when the thing is finally laid out full size.

The next step is to work out how an operational sequence would run. This is really a large separate subject, but, in a nutshell, you need to establish that what you have sketched out actually does what you

Tip

Look closely at the prototype locomotives running in your chosen prototype model area. Are they available RTR, or would they need to be kit-built? If it is the latter and you are not confident about building locomotives from kits, it may be better to choose another general area rather than get frustrated later on if what you end up with is too compromised.

want it to do and provides enough interest. Small, perfectly formed and highly accurate layouts can look lovely, but if the operation only involves running a 48XX and an auto-trailer in and out, then the whole exercise will last little more than a week before it is abandoned. The final operation of your layout in its finished form is likely to have more of a bearing on its success and longevity than any matter of modelling skill.

TIMETABLES AND SEQUENCING

Take another piece of paper and write out around twenty moves (about one hour's model operation). Number them 1–20 and add 24-hour clock times to them, starting with '5.55 milk train' for instance, and finishing with a 21.00 last passenger. Flesh this out a little with possible traffics, but don't get too carried away with goods traffic. A line like this would generate no more than three goods trains a day at the absolute maximum; probably only one and then only on Monday, Wednesday and Friday.

Within this exercise it is also worth thinking about the surroundings. Is it a farming area? Is it a coastal holiday area? Is there any local manufacturing? How would this affect the traffic? Ashburton, for example, took very little passenger traffic in its latter years, but the cattle-train frequency was way beyond what you would first imagine due to the rural nature of the line. On the other hand, St Ives was (and still is) almost totally geared toward holiday traffic, so the feel is

reversed. All of these aspects add to making your layout feel real, by giving reason for the operation and lifting it away from a series of random movements.

THE LIGHT RAILWAY IDEA

The light railway scenario is another which is not quite as obvious, especially if you are new to the game. The plan shows a fairly typical layout, with a loop and two sidings inspired by New Radnor, The Tanant Valley Railway and Dinas Mawddwy. The stock that would be used for this is both short and small, which is a bonus for those short of space, but don't fall into the trap of thinking that this is necessarily a small layout. The GWR's absorbed light railways were in out of the way rural areas and built on reasonably cheap farmland, so tended to sprawl somewhat in ground terms. To get the correct vibe, a feel of open space should be foremost in your mind when planning this type of layout.

Light Railways

The GWR absorbed several light railways either at or before the 1923 Grouping. Some lines that we regard as the 'classic' GWR branch lines were originally built using independent finance under the British Government's 1896 Light Railway Act. This was ostensibly designed to open up rural areas to trade by allowing a rail line to be built more cheaply than normal and with slightly less regulation than would ordinarily be the case. The downside was that although a lighter approach to signalling was allowed, there was usually a corresponding reduction in permitted axle weights and maximum speeds – often no more than 25mph. In most instances, the GWR continued to use the existing locomotive stock of the line after takeover, then phased in its own small engine fleet such as the lighter weight pannier tanks or the 517/48XX types. That these restricted weight/speed lines were often the saving grace of many of the ex-commuter engines that had become redundant in their original urban homes.

Dinas Mawddwy station site, still showing the remains of the platform. The station building is now a private dwelling, but the rest of this light railway terminus site has been cleared and is now a craft centre.

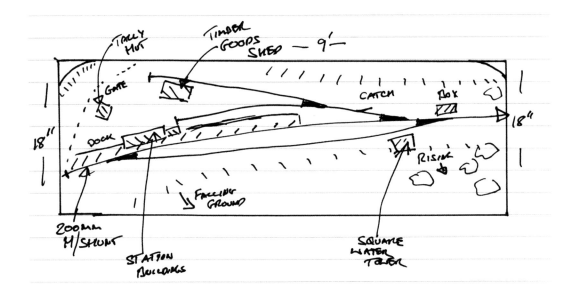

GWR - LIGHT RAILWAY

Sketch of possible GWR absorbed light railway showing typical track layout.

TAKING THE MINIMALIST APPROACH

For those modellers with little or no room, there is a possibility to take one step further in compression. The micro layout has gained popularity in recent years and this may be the route to take if space is extremely limited. Operation is not a big factor here, but if your main interest is building items of stock and you wish to have somewhere to display and photograph them, this could be an ideal move.

The GWR provided numerous tiny halts on branch lines, initially for use with steam rail-motors. The platforms were short – usually between 50–150ft (15,240–45,720mm) long – and the facilities were minimal, often only a pagoda type waiting shelter or something less stylish, or even sometimes no shelter at all.

Some of these halts featured a short siding for local produce to be loaded, and one such siding is included here, giving a modicum of light operational worth. But if your interest is in running trains, this

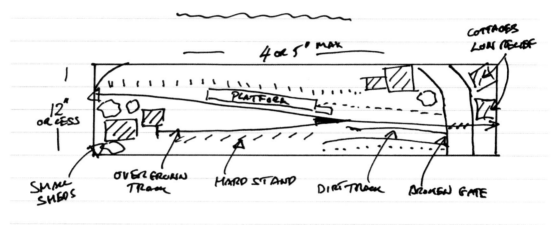

Sketch of possible minimum space GWR halt.

Whitehall Halt on the Culm Valley line. This shot from the balcony of the brake van in 1959 shows the tiny platform on the right. A short siding ran from just past the bridge to a point between the mill and the gate on the left. A similar scene would involve lot of modelling, but would take up a tiny amount of space even in O gauge. MICHAEL FARR

will not be the layout for you. If, however, you want a small project to test a few new scenic techniques, this type of micro layout does have applications beyond being something that is to be used for running. For example, if you wished to try your hand at building your own track, such a piece would be ideal, as the parameters are set tightly and you would not feel that the time was wasted if you then found that it was not for you.

MOVING ON

So, with all this planning carried out, what's next? At this point, if you have not done so already (and still assuming 4mm scale OO), it would be a good

time to purchase a small locomotive. One from the list on the sketches would be a good idea. A pannier tank is an ideal first GWR locomotive purchase, as it will fit anywhere on the central section, as will the 48XX. A 45XX prairie tank would be a fair bet for a first loco to do the same branch work in the West Country. The Dean Goods could have appeared anywhere excepting the far west of Wales, where something built for the Cambrian Railway would be more logical. This single locomotive purchase may be all you need for quite a period of time, giving you enough to test things and to drag some rolling stock around your new layout. From this point, you can build things up slowly and carefully.

CHAPTER TWELVE

EXHIBITING YOUR GWR BRANCH LAYOUT

EXHIBITING YOUR GWR LAYOUT

Sooner or later, either when a layout has just been started or is nearly finished, the question arises of whether to take it to model railway exhibitions or not. In some ways, this is the worst possible time to make this decision, as there are very marked differences between the home-based layout and one that is taken out and shown to the public at one of the many model railway exhibitions held up and down the country. As mentioned earlier, the way that a layout is designed at a basic level affects its functionality as an exhibition piece.

Here are a few things to consider, probably even before drawing your first pencil plan. Some of these can cause a degree of argument amongst modellers, but, as is often the case, the advice is to build your model in a way that suits you, and only you, and stick with this until you find something better. Along the way, you will get given opinions – some positive, some negative – and most of them not asked for or needed.

HOME OR EXHIBITION?

There is one particular modeller who works in 3mm scale who states that whenever he is asked to exhibit his home layout, he screws it ever more firmly to the wall. To some, modelling is a very private affair and even though they are happy to share ideas and photos of their models via magazine articles, or these days more than likely via various Internet forums and blogs, they are unwilling to participate in a public show. This is a sound argument; it is often overlooked that in exhibiting a layout at a public show, we are entering a minor branch of the entertainment business, and to pretend that this isn't so is pure folly. We may be mixing with like-minded souls who understand and like what we do, but that is no different to saying that an actor starring in a West End musical shares with his audience a liking for show tunes. There is a venue, a ticket to enter and the visitors expect a quality show and an hour or so of enjoyment for which they have paid. Showing your layout is not to be taken lightly. It will be praised, criticized and, through handling, will probably gain some damage along the way. And, for these reasons, if you have any doubts as to whether this is acceptable to you, it is probably safe to say that a home layout shared through magazine articles or over the Internet is by far the best route.

That said, there are many advantages to showing your layout. Firstly, there is the friendship gained from mixing with like-minded people, especially if part of a model railway club. Some exhibitions organize social events after the close, where exhibitors can discuss the day and reflect on what went well and what didn't. Secondly, there is the chance to act as a salesman for your particular branch of the hobby, whether it be the Great Western Railway modelling in general, or your particular chosen scale/gauge combination. Contact details can be exchanged across the layout and new relationships struck, with often a mutual exchange of relevant material, as an exhibition visitor may have an out of print book that holds a drawing, a piece of information that you have found hard to locate, or may even have direct experience of the line you are modelling. Even with a large library and the Internet, there is always a scrap of information that is annoyingly missing.

Thirdly, there is of course the pleasure of showing your modelling work and getting an instant reaction to it and possibly many questions, especially if you have employed an unusual technique to produce a certain item. Again, this can lead to a conversation which may point you toward a new construction material, or a new source for an old one that seems to have vanished. In short, exhibiting your layout has an awful lot going for it. So how does this affect what and how you build?

FRONT OR REAR OPERATION?

One of the fundamental questions is always: Is the operator going to work the layout from the front or the back? With a home layout, this question does not usually arise, as the baseboard will nearly always be placed against, or mounted on, one of the household walls, so it is usually only possible to operate from the front; you are in essence both viewer and operator at the same time. With an exhibition layout, you have to decide which it is to be, and you have to decide quite early on in the planning period.

Each operating position has its pluses and minuses. The front position puts you close to the public and therefore in an increased communicative position. It does mean that you are either standing directly in front of the scene that the public wishes to view, or slightly to one side of it, where being able to see if rolling stock has cleared points properly or uncoupled becomes difficult, due to the shallow angle of vision. There is also the problem of the public being so close that any manual adjustment becomes tricky, as they may be standing in the way. Barriers are often provided at larger shows, but these can introduce a whole other raft of problems and push the public even further away from you. Rear operation provides less public interaction, as the layout can act as a barrier, especially if there is a high proscenium arch or lighting rig attached to it, which can block eye contact. The main advantage of rear operation is that the operator has a completely unobstructed working space along the entire layout and can move freely along this to gain the best viewpoint for effective operation. without having to elbow crowds of people out of the way if an item of stock has become derailed. It also means that point and signal control and other switching equipment can be hidden at the rear, giving a clean and uncluttered front face to the layout.

The usual way to build an exhibition layout is to have it operated from the rear in traditional theatre style.

Either of these operation positions is valid and it is very much up to the builder which he or she finds most comfortable. This is really the crux of the matter, as it is the operator who is standing there for six to seven hours during the course of an exhibition, not the visitor, who may only linger for a minute or two before moving on to something else. It is this factor above all which should be the primary consideration. You are building for you, not for someone who watches for a few seconds, never to return, although hopefully you will attract large crowds that watch the layout through an entire running sequence. Constructing an exhibition layout that is highly popular, but leaves you with backache throughout the following day, is never going to be pleasurable, no matter how well the modelling is executed.

HIGH, LOW OR SOMEWHERE IN THE MIDDLE?

It there is one subject that gets the blood pressure rising, it is the thorny question of exhibition layout heights. The blame for this can certainly be laid at the feet of a book by Iain Rice, *An Approach to Model*

Front operation is less popular, but it does make contact with the audience far easier. Note the high quality of presentation here, with full display framing, drapes and information sheets mounted at the front.

Lighting need not be complex; here Giles Barnabe uses low-voltage Christmas tree light wrapped around a simple frame. These give out an ideal wash of light, but are invisible from normal viewing angles.

Railway Layout Design, which considered all aspects of layout design. Before the publication of this in the early 1990s, the usual traditional layout position was at a height roughly comparable to a standard domestic table. Iain suggested through a series of diagrams that the most natural way to view a model railway was at eye level, as this was the angle at which we viewed the real thing. The result of this is that gradually exhibition layouts have grown in stature – some just a little, but there are some notable examples set where the man of average height is looking slightly up at them. This is all very well, until you consider that not all of society has a standing eye level of 5ft (1,524mm) and a proportion of them are not standing at all. Needless to say, these high-set layouts get a volley of complaints from those who are wheelchair-bound or otherwise unable to see.

It is clear that in the end it is impossible to please all, but that a lower to mid-height is more likely to satisfy the majority. For example, the author's standard exhibition layout height setting is around 1,090mm from track level to the floor. This enables an eye-level view for wheelchair users

and children, but does not mean that the operators or those of above average height have to stoop too much.

Although the height of a layout is not super-critical at the design stage, it is worth thinking about how it will be viewed, and from what angle, as this can have a bearing on the position of some buildings and the disguising of exit points. Of course, if the layout is home-based, you have no one to please but yourself, but if there is the chance that it will be exhibited, then these height or front/back matters can make or break a good layout. The best way to decide on these matters is to visit a few model railway exhibitions and see how you feel about the height of each one and also watch the public reaction to it.

PRESENTATION

Developing almost parallel to the rising layout heights has been the development in layout presentation. Once again, pre-1990s a layout was usually presented either sat on a trestle table, or on legs of a similar height to this, with often unpainted timber facing and nothing to indicate what it was. If it was in

Model railway exhibitions have become highly professional affairs and are a mix of layouts and trade stands.

a dark corner of the hall, the visitors would have difficulty seeing it, as it would probably be lacking in any independent lighting. Contrast that image to those of the exhibitions of the twenty-first century and you will find much has changed. Layouts now resemble the most professional of commercial trade stands, have name boards, drapes and often complex fluorescent and LED lighting arrangements, combined with a proscenium arch over the top; the attitude to presentation has shifted significantly.

Although this is not specific to Great Western layouts, it is necessary to point out that all this needs to be considered along with the height question when building your layout. These days, it is simply not acceptable to wander into an exhibition without some sort of drapes to cover the stand legs and, at the very least, a rudimentary lighting set-up. These need not be expensive and it is also worth pointing out that low-voltage kitchen-unit type lights have made it possible to keep mains-rated power away from the upper regions of the layout. Once again, it is time well spent viewing layouts at exhibitions and asking the builders how and why they have used a particular set-up, then working out if you can do something similar.

MONEY

Finally, there is the question of money. Most exhibitions offer some degree of compensation in the form of cash expenses, which are normally presented an hour or so before the show closes. These expenses would cover fuel costs, vehicle hire and possible accommodation costs if the exhibitor has paid for these upfront. Although this payment should not have any bearing on what you build, if you are hoping to exhibit, it is worth considering how you will transport your layout and how much this will cost. For example, looking at whether you can alter the board design so that it and all the support systems will fit into the family car (with all the rolling stock, power supplies and spare operator), is going to be far better than having to factor in van hire to move it to the venue. An exhibition manager is naturally looking at the ratio of floor space to cost, so if you turn up with a very small badly packed layout and then demand van-hire charges there will almost certainly be problems. Although normally the idea is not for the modeller to profit financially, there is the necessity to meet the organizers at least halfway and it is best to sort these issues out at the point of the layout being booked. To this end, most well-run club exhibitions require a paper or digital form to be filled in that outlines all of the possible size/transport/expense issues in one fell swoop.

The amounts charged can vary and once again some subtle questions in the right ears will give the answer to what is and is not generally acceptable to all parties. A small village hall show is just not going to generate enough ticket income to cover expensive layouts in the same way as a major exhibition hall show, so this needs to be taken into consideration when you take the booking. The Lesser Deeping Model Railway Society exhibition held in Deeping village hall is unlikely to be able to find the money for two days of van hire and hotel accommodation for the operators, so some serious 'meeting them halfway' will be needed.

CHAPTER THIRTEEN

CONCLUSIONS

If you have read this far, that's great, and if you have had a go at some of the individual projects contained in the book, that's even better. Many books are a thinly veiled set of personal opinions that the reader is supposed to buy into. Although there are a couple of personal takes on certain aspects, there has been so much written about the GWR beforehand that it would be sheer folly to try to either change that, or to try to rewrite any of it. The main thrust of this book is to try to get the complete novice or someone with only a limited amount of experience to have a go, and at the very least attempt some railway modelling beyond opening the box of an RTR item of rolling stock. There is also an awareness that no matter how long you pursue this engaging lifelong hobby, there is always a degree of lack of confidence – people are frightened of messing something up and wasting the time and money. There is only one thing worse than this, which is buying kits and RTR models and then making no attempt to take the process any further; the classic 'armchair modeller'. In some ways, buying this book will not change a large percentage of these people and it will join many others like it on a shelf and have no effect on any modelling progress – unless the book is regarded as pure entertainment, the money spent on it will also have been wasted.

BASEBOARDS AND SCENERY

What has not been covered within these pages is baseboard construction and general scenic techniques. This was seen as being fairly superfluous, as baseboards are the same for any model railway – one featuring the Great Western Railway or not. There are a couple of fine books on the subject available from The Crowood Press and it is suggested that you investigate these and others should you need some assistance and inspiration. The same goes for general

Scenic items for the GWR layout can include some of the company's numerous road vehicles.

Small and highly compressed scenes can be a feature of many GWR layouts.

scenery advice – most of it is non-GWR specific and there are always plenty of magazine articles available and again if a book is required there are several dealing with various aspects of scenic work in this publisher's series.

WORKING TO A BUDGET

The idea throughout this book has not only been to encourage some model-making, but there has also been a subtext of encouraging a large degree of low-cost budget modelling, or, more to the point, making things for oneself. This is really a subject all on its own, but the use of older or second-hand materials covers two bases. Firstly, it reduces the fear of messing up, as a cheap second-hand model holds less emotional value than something shiny, brand-new and expensive. Secondly, this approach gently leads the modeller to grow in confidence; we are generally led to believe that if we buy an expensive brand-new RTR model, we have reached the pinnacle of excellence, but in reality we have only spent and not improved. What simply buying a model definitely will not do is raise the confidence of the individual modeller, as there is a feeling of 'I won't be able to reach that standard'. By taking a lesser quality or older model in whatever scale and adding something to it, even if it is just some

coal in a locomotive bunker, we have put something of ourselves into it – it is no longer just *a model*, but now becomes *my model*. And it is that sense of pride and ownership that cannot be bought at any price, no matter if the resulting quality is high or not.

SIDEWAYS THINKING

Aside from encouraging the novice modeller to do more for themselves, the other main aim of this book has been gently to push the modeller to think slightly outside of the box in terms of purchasing. In other words, don't blindly accept what is thrown at you without question. All the way through the text, points have been made about glib and convenient mislabelling of RTR models. These should be the first set of questions that you ask: How realistic do I wish it to be? And, does this model box or set of kit parts actually reflect this and meet my hoped for standard? Conversely, the questions may be: Do I really need to buy this? Can I make this myself? Or, can this box of kit parts, which is labelled for something else, be adapted to create something that is accurate (or pretty close) to something purely Great Western?

It is questions like these which in general terms set the thinking railway modeller apart from someone who simply has a train set. The 100 per cent accuracy ideal may never be achieved – and that doesn't really matter – but the aim for something more accurate and fulfilling will now be firmly fixed as part of the modeller's mental toolbox.

THE GWR CLICHÉ

Choosing the GWR is a very smart move in a lot of ways, as many of the hurdles that may be there in modelling for other prototype railway companies are swept away. Most of what you need can initially be bought easily and cheaply at new prices and, because of the popularity, the second-hand availability is second to none. Try finding cheap second-hand LMS coaches to work on and you will be looking for quite a while, but look for GWR B-set coaches and they are there on nearly every second-hand stand at every model railway exhibition. There should now be little or no fear in improving them, as there is simply nothing to lose.

Is modelling the GWR branch line a cliché, though? Well, that, like most things in life, depends on who you ask. The question here is whether there is any difference between something that is regarded as a cliché and something that is regarded as popular? The model companies have pushed the Great Western Railway in their product ranges and the public have reacted by buying it. You could say that if they hadn't put their hands in their pockets to pay for the goods, the model manufacturers would have tried another angle – it's a chicken and egg argument. Whatever the answer is, there is no doubt of the GWR's continuing popularity, both as a matter of general interest and as a modelling subject. By buying this book, you have only further confirmed this line of thinking.

The term 'cliché' is often levelled at the GWR branch line in model form by those in argumentative and competitive mood – it is in reality a type of snobbery. However, what is notable is that some of the finest models on the exhibition circuit are based on GWR prototypes. There does, in fact, seem to be no lack of enthusiasm for the GWR from some of the most skilled and respected amateur and professional

Andy Cundick's delightful early style wooden outside-framed brake van.

modellers. What this certainly illustrates is that the subject is so deep and absorbing that even these highly motivated modellers can continue to find both interest in the prototype subject and enough modelling to make it worth spending hours and possibly years digging into the fine detail; a detail level that shows no sign of being exhausted. The long historical dateline of the Great Western Railway means that if you so wished you could even build a series of GWR layouts over a lifetime, possibly working backwards from a post-World War II scene, through the late 1930s, the 1920s, the Edwardian period and into the broad-gauge years, with only minimal crossover with regard to rolling stock. That's five broad periods, five model scenes, five sets of rolling stock and five sets of passenger fashions to work through, without resorting to any great geographical shifts. If you are highly confident, even the broad gauge could be split into two defined periods – pre-mixed gauge and post-mixed gauge.

In other words, if buying this book is your very first step toward building a Great Western Railway branch-line model, then regardless of any successes and catastrophes along the way, the interest will probably remain with you for a lifetime.

INDEX